# Antivirus For Your Mind

How to Strengthen Your
Persistence and Determination
and Feel Good More Often

## Adam Khan

ISBN: 0962465623
ISBN-13: 978-0962465628



Published in the USA

YouMe Works Publishing

# TABLE OF CONTENTS

# ACKNOWLEDGMENTS

Reading the book, *Learned Optimism*, by Martin Seligman, twenty years ago opened my eyes to a whole new world. I would like to thank Martin Seligman, David Burns, Julian Simon, and Albert Ellis for their seminal contributions to the field.

# THE HEART OF THE MATTER

Right now you spend a certain percentage of your life feeling negative emotions — nervous, frustrated, sad, angry, worried, whatever. I don't know what the percentage is. One percent of your waking hours? Five percent? Ten percent? Whatever it is, the information in this book can help you lower it. You will spend less of your time feeling badly and more of your time feeling good.

And you will not only feel good, you'll also become more capable of achieving your goals. The same thing that causes bad feelings also makes you less competent, less creative, and less energetic. It also makes you less persistent, less determined, and more likely to give up on a goal.

And as if that wasn't enough, those negative feelings are bad for your health.

What causes all these things? What harms your health, impairs your ability, and makes you feel unnecessary, unpleasant emotions? One simple thing: Making lousy explanations of setbacks.

When you experience a setback of any kind, you explain it. This is one of the most important discoveries ever made by psychology. When you hit a setback, you *will* explain it. You can't help it. The reaction is totally automatic. And your explanation is about what *caused* the setback.

For example, let's imagine one morning, right after you get dressed for work, you spill coffee on your white shirt. This is a small setback. (A setback is something you wanted to happen that didn't happen, or something you didn't want to happen that happened.)

After you spill coffee on your shirt, you will *automatically* explain to yourself *why* it happened. How many explanations do you think are possible? Here are a few possible explanations:

- I am so clumsy!

- I must have been distracted.

- I am moving too fast.

- I've got too much going on in my life and I can't handle it.

- I can't do anything right!

As you can see, the possible explanations for this simple setback are almost endless. And as you can also see, the *emotional* impact of each explanation can differ quite a bit. You might feel it is no big deal, or you might feel terribly upset about the incident, depending on how you explain it to yourself.

This fact has important practical implications — very direct and significant practical implications. What do I mean? Just this: Some explanations help you and some impair you. If you think, "I am moving too fast," and you slow down a little, that might help. You might prevent further accidents.

But if you think you can't do anything right, you might not slow down, you might feel upset at that "fact," so you might make *more* mistakes.

That particular explanation not only made you feel bad, but "I can't do anything right" implies you are helpless to change it. That is the worst kind of explanation you can make if it's not true — and it almost never is.

The very same event can cause one person to be motivated to change something, and another to feel defeated and helpless, depending on how they explain the setback to themselves.

The reason this simple fact has tremendous implications is because you and I experience many setbacks every single day. How many days do you have when *everything* goes exactly the way you want?

Because of the habitual way you explain setbacks, you usually have a feeling of motivation and confidence...or a feeling of discouragement, and the feeling accumulates day after day. In the long run, the way you explain setbacks to yourself determines, to an astonishing degree, how your life will turn out.

Successfully losing weight depends on how you explain setbacks to yourself. If you want to lose weight and you've just finished eating too much, this little setback can make you want to give up on your goal to lose weight, or it can make you more determined than ever — depending on how you explain your "failure" to yourself.

If you try to improve your marriage and your efforts at communicating cause an argument, it can make you want to throw in the towel or it can make you want to try *harder* — depending on how you explain this setback.

If you try to lower the level of stress in your life but your efforts only seem to cause you *more* stress, it can make you feel defeated *or* motivated — depending on how you explain the setback to yourself.

## a good explanation

What makes an explanation good or bad? This is the crucial question. Here is the answer: It is a good explanation if it doesn't have a lot of mistakes in it. A bad explanation is one that contains mistakes. We will go into much greater detail about that in a minute.

But first, where do our block-headed explanations come from? How can a perfectly reasonable person like yourself make explanations bad enough to make you feel bad unnecessarily?

Bad explanations spring out of four sources:

> 1. Your brain's naturally-occurring flaws some-times lead you to explain your setbacks badly.

2. You picked up some of your explanations of setbacks from what you've heard others say.

3. Sometimes just the nature of reality itself can give you a false impression.

4. And of course, the intense flood of negative input from media sources can (and does) influence the way you explain setbacks.

Those influences enter your mind from many sources just as a virus can enter your computer from an email, from a website, or from a flashdrive a friend gave you.

Wherever your "mind viruses" come from, once they enter your mind, they can infect you with a negative attitude, ruining your mood, harming your health, impairing your ability to act in your own best interest, and making it harder to succeed.

If you learn how to improve your explanations, you can be more successful at *everything* — your relationships with your children, your job, your golf game, and so on — and why? Because you are far more effective when you feel *determined and motivated* than when you feel demoralized (or any other negative emotion). You are more effective and you're more likely to try again.

And as you can see, this doesn't only apply to the big career-busting or heart-rending setbacks. We all experience many smaller setbacks every day.

We call "everyday setbacks" by other names, such as irritation, frustration, disappointment, annoyance, having a problem, running into trouble, etc.

The small letdowns and difficulties are each a *set-back* that either makes you feel motivated or makes you feel a negative emotion, depending on what you have decided *caused* the setback.

Below are some examples of everyday setbacks. Notice that some of them don't take the form of an obvious setback. That's important to remember:

- Your wrist ached today for no apparent reason.

- Your boss seemed sullen and distant when you tried to talk to her.

- You have felt tired a lot lately.

- You've gone two weeks without smoking but today you smoked a cigarette.

- You want to cut down on junk food but you haven't done it yet.

- You've been trying to think more positively, but it hasn't been working.

- Your son doesn't seem to want to talk to you anymore.

- You're not as attractive to the opposite sex as you once were.

A setback is doing worse than you expected. Remember, a setback is something you wanted to happen that didn't happen, or something you didn't want to happen that happened.

Each of the setbacks above could be motivating, energizing, and fill you with determination...or the very same setback could make you feel bad, *depending on what you automatically decided caused the setback.*

# MOMENT OF TRUTH

In 1934, Admiral Byrd was feeling demoralized, and for good reason. He was dying of carbon monoxide poisoning without knowing it. All he knew was he was sick and getting sicker. Byrd was stationed at a remote base deep in the interior of Antarctica, about as removed from civilization as a person can get on this planet. He was utterly alone and, he thought, without hope of rescue. That's a setback by definition (he was doing worse than he expected). When Byrd arrived at the base camp, he had expected to make it home alive, of course, and now it looked like he would never make it.

He gave up. He was going to die, he admitted to himself. This is how it would end. He wrote a note to the people who would find his body the following spring and then snuffed out the candles. He lay in the dark for some time, sad at this horrible turn of fate.

But then he remembered a scene from his past. He had been in a wrestling match, trying to win the championship at the Naval Academy. Near the end of the match, exhausted and in great pain, he decided he had no chance of winning.

But his mother was watching and he wanted her to be proud of him, so he spontaneously invented a technique, and it worked. He stumbled onto the secret of determination. He *immediately* felt his strength resurge and he fought to the finish.

It worked then, he thought, so it might work here in the Antarctic even though his situation was now incomparably worse.

The single thought that revived him in the wrestling match was the realization that "although I seemed absolutely washed up, there was a chance I was mistaken."

That's the most important key to pulling out of a negative emotion: Admit to yourself you might be mistaken about a pessimistic conclusion. Introduce some doubt.

The doubt is legitimate. Most of us are far more confident in our negative assumptions than is justified by the facts. As Norman Cousins put it, "Nobody knows enough to be a pessimist."

In the gripping true story, *In the Heart of the Sea: The Tragedy of the Whaleship Essex*, two people died within 24 hours of deciding their situation was hopeless. Yet many made it home alive. It was a premature decision (they *decided* there was no hope of making it back home), and in this case, their demoralization made them as incapable as a person can become: It killed them.

Hopelessness sucks out your determination.

In the same story, on the other hand, is an example of suddenly feeling that some effort might make a difference. They spotted land. A minute before, they were all lying there, demoralized, waiting to die, without energy, without hope. Suddenly they saw land, and these wasted, dehydrated, starving, helpless men were suddenly filled with energy as they scrambled to propel their boat toward shore.

One minute before, *although their dire circumstances were real,* the hopelessness was in their minds, which means it was changeable.

Just one minute before, their circumstances were essentially the same, and yet, they were demoralized and had no energy because of their conviction that their situation was hopeless. It was a conviction they held with more confidence than they should have.

This is an example of the difference between feeling demoralized and feeling determined. You are far more powerful and *capable* when you feel motivated than when you feel discouraged. And those feelings arise from the way you're explaining the setback.

If your explanation is pure guesswork, as it often is, it's stupid to stick with a guess that demoralizes you. Introduce some doubt. It is the only sane thing to do.

Pessimistic thinking is almost always a mistake. Not only is it a mistake because it makes you less capable, but the thoughts *themselves* are usually in error. I'll have a lot more to say about that in a minute. But for now, just be aware that making a mistake in your explanation of a setback can make you feel defeated, overwhelmed, or beaten when you aren't any such thing.

I'm not sure you really *got* that, and it is crucial you do. Please read the following sentence slowly and carefully:

*Making a mistake in your explanation of a setback can make you feel defeated, overwhelmed, or beaten when you aren't any such thing.*

Mistakes in your explanations can take away your fight, suck out your desire, and kill your determination. Mistaken explanations can stop you from taking action. If your thought-mistakes fool you into believing you can do nothing about a difficulty, *you will do nothing.* This is hazardous to your goals!

If you explain a setback to yourself in a way that makes you feel bad, you can change your explanation. Even if you're in the habit of explaining setbacks in a way that demoralizes you, you're not stuck with that habit. You can change it.

You can *improve* the way you explain setbacks. It's not hard to do, and it will make a huge difference if you do.

Even if you already make pretty good explanations, making better ones will make you even *more* difficult to demoralize than you are now. You will feel better and get more done. You'll have less negative emotion and you'll be more effective with your actions.

# LEARNERS WILL INHERIT
# THE EARTH

You have opportunities to become more capable — on the job, in your relationships, in just about anything and everything you do. Opportunities to learn come up all the time. And becoming more capable makes you feel good about yourself, increases your motivation, and gives you confidence.

And how does a person become more capable? By overcoming obstacles and persisting with goals. There is no other way.

Okay then, how do you become more persistent? Not by willpower. Are you listening to me? The hard way to become more persistent is by sheer willpower. It is difficult and tends to be short-lived. The easy way — and the way that makes you lastingly stronger and feel better too — is by improving the way you explain setbacks to yourself.

If you are trying to find love, for example, the explanations you make of your setbacks will determine how successful your search will be (and how much fun you'll have doing it).

When a shy young man asks a girl out on a date and she turns him down, will he ask her again (or ask someone else)? Or will he decide he's a loser, that he'll *never* get a date, that nobody loves him, etc. How things eventually turn out for him depends quite a bit on how he explains setbacks like these. He could become a withdrawn adult who aches to have a close relationship but never does. Or he could rise to the challenge, learn what he needs to learn, and persist, and become happily married.

Good explanations of setbacks and bad explanations of setbacks both tend to become self-fulfilling prophesies that accumulate evidence to support them as life rolls along.

So do you want to feel better and accumulate evidence that you are capable? Would you like things to go your way more often? Of course you would! All you need to do is think differently.

# CAN'T WE JUST AVOID EXPLAINING SETBACKS?

Explaining setbacks can get you into trouble. So can't we simply avoid explaining setbacks altogether? Good question. It seems like the obvious solution, right? To avoid making mistakes in your explanations, *simply avoid making explanations.* There is only one problem with this answer: It is impossible.

Wait a minute. Am I being unnecessarily defeatist? No. Please don't go off the deep end of optimism by concluding that nothing is impossible. Some situations *are* hopeless and some things *are* impossible. And one of those things is preventing your mind from explaining setbacks. Let me illustrate the problem with a few research tidbits.

Researchers sprayed androstenol on half the chairs in a waiting room. Androstenol is chemically related to male sex hormones. It stimulates a particular nerve in the nose, but has no odor. Women coming into the waiting room tended to sit in the sprayed seats, and men tended to avoid sitting in them.

But here's the interesting part: Each person was asked, "Why did you choose to sit in that particular chair?"

Their answers had nothing to do with smelling anything. They said things like, "I wanted to read, so I sat by the magazines," or "it was closest to the door."

Neither the men nor the women had any idea their decision was influenced by androstenol. And yet clearly it was.

But they had no problem answering the question about why they sat where they sat, and even though their answers were plausible, they were wrong. Isn't that interesting? Why do you suppose they answered the way they did? Why didn't they just say, "I don't know?"

Because they (and you and I) have an automatically-functioning explanation-producing part of our brain. It takes whatever information we're aware of and makes the most plausible explanation, and it does this whether we want it to or not.

In another study, a different group of researchers told their subjects something like this, "John is a man who ran away from home as a child. Now he is in the Peace Corps. Can you explain how the childhood incident could account for the fact that John decided to join the Peace Corps?"

The subjects were easily able to explain it plausibly.

A different set of subjects were told, "John is a man who ran away from home as a child. He recently committed suicide. Can you explain how the childhood incident could account for the fact that John decided to commit suicide?"

And again, the subjects had no problem at all coming up with plausible explanations.

It reminds me of an example I heard from Earl Nightingale. Twin boys grew up with an alcoholic father. As adults, one of the brothers was an alcoholic and the other never drank. In separate interviews, each was asked, "Why did you turn out the way you did?"

Both brothers gave exactly the same answer: "With a father like mine, what else would I be?"

Several experiments have shown that if you give someone a test and then say, "Based on this test, we have determined you are above average at reading," and then ask the person to explain it, they can explain it very well.

What the researchers discovered is that it doesn't matter if the subject is told, "You're *above* average at reading," or "You're *below* average at reading." If people believe the result was from a legitimate test, they can explain it. And explain it *believably*.

And it didn't matter what the researchers tested for. If they could lead the subject to believe he or she was above or below average at *anything*, that person was able to explain it — plausibly.

## a hypnotic experiment

Two people sit in a room. One is the researcher. The other is a volunteer who is hypnotized and given a post-hypnotic suggestion: After he awakens from the trance, says the experimenter, the volunteer will respond a particular way to a specific thing. Let's say the volunteer is told, "When I say 'it's a nice day today,' you will get up, open the door, and look down the hall. But you will not remember that I gave you this instruction."

The volunteer is awakened and the two talk casually for a few minutes. Then the researcher nonchalantly says, "It's a nice day today."

The volunteer gets up, opens the door, and looks down the hall. He comes back and sits down. The researcher asks, "Why did you do that?"

The volunteer says, "It's stuffy in here. I'm letting in some air."

The researcher closes the door and they continue talking for a few minutes, and again, the researcher says, "It's a nice day today."

And again, the volunteer gets up, opens the door and looks down the hall.

"Why did you open the door again?" asks the researcher.

The volunteer says, "I thought I heard a noise outside."

This experiment has been repeated many times with different volunteers, always with the same result. People follow the post-hypnotic suggestion and when asked, come up with a plausible reason for their own behavior — a reason that in fact had nothing to do with it.

Again we see there is a part of the brain that just seems to generate explanations — wrong, right, and everywhere in between, whether or not it has anything to do with the actual cause of the event.

One more example. For years, a particular kind of epilepsy was cured by a surgery. The corpus callosum was completely cut. The corpus callosum is a thick bundle of nerve fibers that connect the two hemispheres of the brain. Once it has been cut, the two hemispheres can no longer communicate with each other. They become almost like two separate brains.

After the surgery, the epilepsy stops with no apparent side-effects, except for odd little things once in a while. For example, sometimes the person's right hand tries to do something different than the left hand. One hand tries to pull the pants up and the other tries to pull them down. (The left hemisphere of the brain controls the right hand, and the right hemisphere controls the left hand.)

This is such a unique condition, lots of experiments have been done with these people. One in particular is illuminating: Each subject is shown two pictures at the same time, one to their left visual field (which goes to the right hemisphere) and a different picture to their right visual field (which goes to the left hemisphere). So the two sides of the same person's brain is each shown a different picture, and the two sides have no way of communicating with each other.

For example, a picture of a snow-covered meadow was shown to the left visual field. (Keep in mind that the right hemisphere is nonverbal in most people.)

A picture of a bird claw was shown to the person's right visual field (going to the verbal left hemisphere).

Then the person is shown a big collection of pictures and asked, "Which one of these pictures goes with what you just saw?" Both arms move at the same time — the left hand points to a shovel (to go with the snow). But the right hand points to a picture of a chicken (to go with the claw).

The researchers then asked the person, "Why did you point to two different pictures?" And a plausible explanation comes without hesitation, something like this: "Well, the chicken goes with the claw and you clean out the chicken coop with the shovel."

In other words, the explanation-generating part of the brain is clearly in the left (verbal) hemisphere and it didn't see the snow scene. But it did see what the two hands pointed to and explained it easily, without hesitation.

Now, here's the point of all of this: Your brain makes explanations of events, whether you want it to or not. So you can check your explanations for accuracy, but you do not have the option of just avoiding making explanations. Your mind makes explanations immediately and automatically. You can't stop it.

But you *can* improve it.

# HOW TO IMPROVE YOUR EXPLANATIONS

The best way to improve your explanations of setbacks is simply to search for mistakes in your explanations as they arise in your mind. And the best time to search for mistakes is when you're feeling bad.

Our minds work automatically for the most part — interpreting, concluding, deciding, judging — and it serves us well. We would get bogged down if we tried to analyze every explanation we made. So we're not going to even try to do that. It is completely unnecessary. When things are going well and you feel good, let the good times roll.

But when things are *not* working — when things don't turn out as you hoped, when your mood goes south, when you want to give up on your goal — *that's* the time to search for mistakes!

The easiest way to find mistakes is to write down your demoralizing thoughts and argue with those thoughts on paper. Consider yourself personally challenged by those demoralizing statements and defend yourself. Imagine your *least* favorite person said those statements to you and *find something wrong* with those statements. Find everything wrong with them you can.

Decide right now who your least favorite person is. If you have more than one in mind, just choose one.

Now use a mental image of that person when you're arguing with your thoughts. Imagine *that* person explaining your setback to you (with sneering disdain).

The best way to do this is on paper. Writing your explanations down on paper makes them tangible and gives you something to work with. It is *much* easier than trying to do it in your head.

When a setback occurs, write down something you think *caused* the setback. For example, let's say a proposal of yours has been rejected. You write down what you think caused the setback. In this case, you think, "Nobody likes my ideas." That's one of your explanations. That's one of your negative thoughts. In other words, you think your proposal was rejected *because* nobody likes your ideas.

Now argue with that sentence (on paper). Imagine your least favorite person said to you, "Nobody likes your ideas!" Now look for mistakes in that explanation. You might write something like this: "*Nobody?* That might be an exaggeration. Maybe I'm jumping to conclusions. I really haven't tried *everybody*, and besides, it might not be the *ideas*, it might be the presentation, which could be changed," and so on.

After arguing with your thoughts this way, you can see that really only *sometimes* people don't like your ideas. That is a more accurate appraisal of the real situation. And it is not so devastating or upsetting as the thought, "Nobody likes my ideas."

So you have made your explanation of the setback more accurate and less upsetting.

Being less upset won't make you ecstatic or jump for joy, but that is not our purpose here. The aim is to remove demoralization that shouldn't be there. The aim is to take away a feeling of defeat that is false, un-justifiable, and unreasonable.

Feeling demoralized is debilitating — it handicaps you, so the only time you should ever let yourself feel that way is when you really *are* defeated.

Right now, you sometimes feel demoralized *mis-takenly*. We're going to fix that. It might not make you happy, but it will make you feel bad less often and it will make you more powerful (more capable of accomplishing what you want).

## three little snags

It sounds pretty easy to argue with demoralizing thoughts, but three problems tend to come up when you try. First, negative feelings *seem* to arise on their own *without any thoughts causing them*. That, however, is an illusion.

In fact, your negative feelings were preceded by a thought such as, "Nobody likes my ideas." That ex-planation usually zips through your mind so quickly and so automatically, you don't notice it. All you notice is the effect: The resulting feelings.

The speed and invisibility of your own thoughts is a problem. You will have a difficult time arguing with a thought you don't even know you're thinking!

The reason you don't know what you're thinking when you explain a setback is that some thoughts are so well-practiced — you have thought them so many times — that the thinking goes on in the background of your mind.

You explain certain categories of setback with well-practiced explanations, and then you feel a certain way, and all without even realizing it. As far as you can tell, the setback *itself* made you feel bad. It seems *obvious* that anyone would feel bad. It seems *obvious* that feeling bad is the appropriate response. But it only seems that way because your explanation is so familiar to you, and because it zipped by so quickly. And it zipped by so quickly because you've made that explanation so many times.

I want you to fully understand how well-practiced your explanations are. You have many setbacks every day, all of which you explain to yourself, and you've been doing it since before you can remember.

What happens when you do *anything* several times a day for that many years? What happens is that *you stop being aware you're doing it*. It has gone completely automatic. This would not be a problem if we always made good explanations. But sometimes we make mistakes.

The way we now habitually explain setbacks to ourselves is whatever way we haphazardly got into the habit of doing it when we were younger. We're not necessarily making the best possible explanations we could make, as you'll find out. But now it's automatic, just as you sometimes drive your car automatically. You can carry on a conversation while you drive, allowing your driving (a complex process — just ask any new driver) to happen automatically. And you have not had nearly as much practice driving as you have explaining setbacks to yourself.

Because of all this, knowing what your negative thoughts are (so you can argue with them) can be difficult. The solution to this problem is to *write down* your negative thoughts, and argue with them *on paper.*

Your explanations of setbacks are slippery and hard to get a hold of. They move through your mind with practiced speed. But hold them still by putting them down on paper and you can dissect them more easily.

Your thoughts are more airy than a physical habit, and that's the only thing that makes them seem harder to change. But when you write them down, it makes your thoughts real, physical, and available for scrutiny.

So when you begin to try to improve your explanations of setbacks, the *first* problem you'll run into is that your explanations are well-practiced and move with a lot of speed through your mind, making it hard to know what you're thinking.

The second problem occurs even when you *know* what you are thinking. Here it is: You know what you think, but you believe your thoughts are true.

For example, after his divorce, a man decided, "I am doomed to miserable relationships." His mind is made up. He is *sure* he is right. How can he successfully argue with his demoralizing thoughts? He is defeated before he starts.

He may be *aware* of thinking the pessimistic, defeatist thought, but if he assumes he's correct, he'll make no attempt to argue with his thinking.

The solution to this problem is to look at your thoughts with an already-existing list of "virus definitions" (which I will give you shortly). In other words, you won't try to decide on the spot whether your thoughts are true or not. If you feel bad, you'll write down your thoughts.

Even if you think you're not making any mistakes in your thinking, write down your thoughts if you feel bad. Then look at your thoughts through the filter of the virus definitions. You may be mistaken about your explanation without knowing it. The virus definitions will help you discover whether or not this is the case.

The third problem you'll encounter when you try to argue with your thoughts is not knowing *which* thoughts to argue with. You have a lot of thoughts going through your mind. Which ones do you write down and argue with? It's not as hard as it might seem. We can be very specific about what to look for:

1. something you believe caused the setback

2. a belief that makes you feel bad

Let me give you some examples. Let's say you planned to exercise today, but the day is over, and you are now in bed — and you didn't exercise today. You think about it for a second and conclude, "I have no self-discipline." And you feel like a loser.

That conclusion is what you would argue with. The setback is: You didn't exercise. You're trying to get in shape, and you didn't exercise according to your plan. The thought, "I have no self-discipline" is what you believe *caused* the setback. In other words, the reason you didn't exercise is that you have no self-discipline. That reason is what you would argue with. (You're going to learn how to argue later in this chapter.)

Let's look at another example. You're a freshman in college and you get a failing grade on your first exam, and you feel sad. You *were* enthusiastic but now all the enthusiasm about school has disappeared. That is a setback. Remember, a setback is anything that happens you didn't want to happen. Or anything that does *not* happen that you wanted to happen.

You didn't want a failing grade, so it is a setback. You think, "I don't have what it takes." That is your explanation of why you failed the test. That is what you believe *caused* the setback — it's the reason the setback happened — so that is the thought you write down and argue with: "I don't have what it takes."

A woman who showed up to one of my book-signings stayed afterwards to talk to me. She said she was compulsively perfectionistic, but she considered it a fixed part of her character so she had never tried to change it.

This is a setback. It doesn't *seem* like a setback, perhaps, because it didn't happen suddenly. But she didn't *want* to be a perfectionist. Her explanation implied that she couldn't help it. She was born that way. She thought genetics was the cause of her setback, so that was what she wrote down to argue with.

Another reason it doesn't seem like a setback is that her explanation of the setback probably evolved before she really got a chance to form a goal of being more relaxed (less uptight, less perfectionistic). But listening to her, it was clear she didn't want to be a perfectionist. This implies a goal of being free of that compulsion.

But the goal was never articulated because she thought it was impossible. A lot of goals are like that. You probably have some goals like that yourself. The very second you formed the goal in your mind, you dismissed it because of some explanation. So you formed a goal and hit a setback (in your mind) in the same moment.

Things you "always wished" you could do are in that category. You decided they were hopeless dreams the second you thought of them. They sit there in the back of your mind in a state of suspended animation, and they may have remained that way for the rest of your life. You may *never* have checked those explanations for mistakes.

I had one of those. When I was a kid, I wanted to play the electric guitar. But before I even fully clarified that goal in my mind, I had already killed it: "Electric guitars are really expensive, I would have to learn the acoustic first (and I'm not interested in acoustic guitar), I don't have the patience for music lessons, and besides, *everyone* wants to play the electric guitar (so I'd never be able to play in a band because of too much competition)."

These are conclusions I never examined. They were *self-evident* conclusions as far as I was concerned. Conclusions like this destroy motivation and demote a potentially satisfying purpose to an idle daydream. The battle was over before I even knew a battle was going on.

We largely defeat ourselves. Wise people have been saying this for thousands of years. But cognitive researchers (scientists who study the effect of thoughts on feelings and behavior) have discovered *how* we defeat ourselves.

If you have "always wanted" to play the piano, but you think, "I'm too old now; I should have learned as a child," you slam the door on that possibility just as completely as if you had amputated your hands. But what is stopping you? The only thing stopping you is *your explanation of the setback.*

The setback: You would like to play piano, but you have failed to do so.

The explanation: If you're going to play the piano, you have to start when you're a child, and you're no longer a child, so now you can't play the piano.

Let's look at one more example of a setback and its explanation and then we'll get to the meat of the matter. It is vitally important that you understand these first distinctions. The method I explain in this chapter rests on the solid foundation of you knowing exactly what I mean by "setback" and "explanation of a setback."

Let's say you want to become a teacher but you're afraid of speaking in public. Years have gone by and you've never done anything about it. You feel like a chicken, like you have no backbone, and you're a little ashamed of yourself. That's a setback. In this case, it is something that doesn't happen that you wanted to happen. And you feel bad because you believe it will never happen.

Your explanation of why you're afraid to speak in public is, "I was born shy." That is your explanation of the cause of the setback. That's the reason you're afraid to do it. And that is the thought to write down and argue with.

Okay. Enough examples. Now you know what to look for and what to argue with. When you feel demoralized or some other negative emotion, look for what you think caused the setback. Look for the reason you think the setback happened.

Rooting out negative thoughts — and seeing them for what they are — can eliminate the negative emotions they cause. Successfully arguing against those demoralizing thoughts will undemoralize you. It can, and probably will, make you feel good again. And it will make you stronger, more creative, more persistent, and more capable. And it makes you healthier.

A feeling of frustration or demoralization takes the fun out of your days. So immunizing yourself against demoralization is not only good for you and good for your ability to succeed, it makes life more fun!

It takes a little work, but it's worth it. Some people try to skip the work so they "think positive." Let me be very clear on this point: Arguing with your negative thoughts is *not* positive thinking. If you handle your explanations of setbacks by trying to think more positively, it will not work *nearly* as well as finding out what is really and truly mistaken about your negative thoughts.

This is *not* positive thinking. It is more like anti-defeatist or anti-discouragement thinking. Aim at making fewer *mistakes* in your thinking. This is like an anti-virus program for your mind. It is more fundamental than positive thinking, and also more effective when you feel demoralized.

You're not trying to make yourself *believe* a more positive thought here. You're not even trying to make yourself *believe* your negative thoughts are mistaken. You are trying to find actual, *real* mistakes in your negative thoughts. No convincing is necessary, no "faith" is necessary, and trying to make yourself believe something you don't actually believe is unnecessary.

# WHY NEGATIVE THOUGHTS SEEM SO RIGHT

The negative thoughts you have and your (occasionally mistaken) explanations of setbacks seem completely *natural.* The explanations do not appear in your mind as "A *Possible* Explanation For This Setback." You just seem to "know" what caused the setback, usually without giving it another thought.

Your explanations *feel* natural, but remember this: They only feel natural because you've been thinking that way for a long time. Your explanations are *familiar.* When you change your explanations, when you remove some of the mistakes in your thinking, your new explanations will not feel as natural at first because — and only because — they are unfamiliar. But after a while, they will feel as natural as your old explanations did.

The assumptions that flit through our minds with the greatest of ease and make us feel demoralized are common assumptions like these:

- I blew my diet because I'm a pig with no willpower.

- I didn't exercise this week because I'm lazy.

- I need to face the fact that I'll never be able to do this.

- That's the way the economy is going; it's getting harder and harder to make a living.

- I'm a loser.

- There aren't enough hours in the day.

- I don't have enough motivation.

- I don't have enough self-discipline.

- I'm too old.

- Nothing can be done about it.

- Everything is a hassle.

- Nothing comes easy.

These statements are demoralizing. Do the statements contain mistakes or don't they? We're about to find out. But I cannot emphasize enough we're *not* talking about "looking on the bright side" or trying to cover ugly reality with pretty thoughts.

The fundamental point is that if you think a situation is hopeless and you believe you can't do anything about it, you should look carefully at that assumption because it is usually wrong.

This idea is powerful and effective, and it works with everyday setbacks as well as major disasters.

# DISASTER AT SEA

Dougal Robertson was sailing across the Pacific Ocean in 1972 with his family when three killer whales simultaneously struck their boat. (Orcas often attack a larger whale like that, striking it to stun it. Then they eat it.) The sailboat started sinking — fast! Within minutes, their boat was gone and they found themselves sitting in silence on an empty ocean, completely dazed.

They were in the middle of the Pacific on an inflatable life raft and a little fiberglass dinghy, without a radio, without a homing beacon, and a long way from shipping lanes. The wind and currents were moving in the opposite direction of the nearest land. They had very little food or water.

The thoughts going through Dougal's mind were filled with despair. Why, he thought, had he been so reckless as to endanger his family's life like this? How could he have risked their lives with his selfish desire to educate them in such an unorthodox way?

He himself started sinking — into feelings of despair and hopelessness and guilt as he thought about the loss of his boat, the danger his family was in, and the foolish mistakes he had made.

The situation was grim to say the least, and as Dougal thought about it and felt anguish for putting his family in this situation, he suddenly realized his face was showing his hopelessness.

He thought if he became depressed they would have little chance of surviving. He was the leader. They were all looking to him. His own despair would demoralize them all, and he also knew a defeated person does not do what he needs to do to survive.

Dougal had to rise out of his depression. Driven by the necessity of so great a responsibility, he spontaneously invented the way out.

He had never read a book about cognitive therapy. He didn't know there was such a thing. But he started doing exactly what cognitive therapists teach their clients to do: He debated with his own demoralizing thoughts.

His first thought was, *I shouldn't have brought them out in the ocean.* "But," he argued with himself, "Douglas had grown to manhood in our 18 months at sea. The formerly shy and introspective twins had become interested in the world, had expanded their understanding of other people and had awakened their desire to learn more."

*But I took them out on such an old boat.* "It was of much heavier construction than newer boats, and sank slower than a modern boat would have, allowing us time to get off the boat and safely into the life raft."

*But I have now risked their lives.* "What happened was as unforeseeable as an earthquake or an airplane crash."

Dougal's crash-course in anti-defeatism worked. He revived. His demoralization vanished and was replaced by a firm determination to get his family home safely. He explained the situation frankly to the others and what needed to be done, and they immediately started taking actions that helped them survive.

They spent 38 days on the open ocean in their lifeboat and dinghy, overcoming one obstacle after another without losing heart, and they all made it home alive.

Stories of survival show very clearly the power of arguing with defeatist explanations. You can see the usefulness of the principle in naked relief when shown in such harsh live-or-die circumstances. You can see that the only hope the Robertsons had of making it home alive was to *keep trying.* Giving up meant death. Had they succumbed to despair, the slim chance of survival they had would have vanished as quickly as their sailboat beneath the waves.

# THE FLYING KITTY HAWK BROTHERS

My Grampa Bill lived near Kitty Hawk when he was a kid, and used to go watch the Wright brothers testing their aircraft. One time, because the Wright brothers wanted to shut the mouths of the doubters and improve the accuracy of some of the crazy stuff newspapers were printing about their work, the brothers invited reporters out to Kitty Hawk for a demonstration.

Everything went wrong. It was raining pretty hard and they were having trouble with the engine, so they didn't get a chance to do anything until late afternoon. They made one attempt that day, and although the aircraft got up some speed, it never got off the ground.

The rain didn't let up, so they had to wait two more days before they tried it again. This time they got about seven feet off the ground before the plane crashed.

The next day, a *New York Times* headline said, "FALL WRECKS AIRSHIP." (The negative bias of the news media was in full swing even way back then.)

It was *more than a year* before any more reporters came out to visit.

But the Wright brothers continued their work, as determined as ever. Why? What kept them working when they had so many failures? It all boils down to how they explained the setback to themselves. If they told themselves their goal was impossible, or that they weren't capable, or some other explanation that took the wind out of their sails, they would not have pursued their goal, and they would have disappeared into oblivion. Anybody who explains their own setbacks that way gives up in defeat.

But the explanations the Wright brothers made of their many setbacks must have been more sensible. They must have thought the problems were fixable, because they kept working at it. They must have believed the *cause* of the setbacks could be *changed*. Explanations like these keep people from feeling demoralized in the face of setbacks.

It's not *willpower*. It's the way setbacks are *explained*. Remember that.

Most people think you can force yourself to keep going even when you believe it's hopeless. But when you "know" it's hopeless, you won't force yourself. When you are sure you're defeated, it is irrational to persist.

If you really want a drink of water, and you have an empty glass in your hand, and you can see it is empty, you won't bother to try to take a drink from it. You know it is hopeless, no matter how thirsty you are.

Willpower can't help you change your feeling of hopelessness. But when you feel demoralized, finding a mistake in your explanations can restore your determination almost immediately.

"Through some strange and powerful principle of 'mental chemistry' which she has never divulged," wrote Napoleon Hill in 1937, "Nature wraps up in the impulse of STRONG DESIRE 'that something' which recognizes no such word as impossible, and accepts no such reality as failure."

Nobody knew what "that something" was back then. In a chapter on persistence, Napoleon Hill recommended willpower for persisting after a failure. We now know better.

Nature has divulged her secret to the unremitting efforts of cognitive scientists. It isn't willpower. It is sensible explanations of setbacks that makes people determined and persistent.

*Good explanations* are Nature's secret "something" that gives people strength in the face of obstacles. Those who explain their setbacks *in the least demoralizing way* have the most persistence.

In other words, the way to become more persistent is to make sure you don't jump to demoralizing conclusions about the cause of the setback.

Instead of gritting your teeth and forcing yourself to try again even though you feel it's hopeless, try eliminating the feeling of defeat to begin with and then persist naturally, driven by your desire — which remains undiminished by feelings of defeat.

# AN ASPIRING WRITER
# WITH A SENSIBLE WIFE

A clergyman in his fifties had written the manuscript for a book. Since he lived in New York City, where most publishers were back in those days, he spent his spare time going into publishers' offices and asking them to look at his manuscript. Nobody was interested.

It can, of course, be disheartening to get rejection after rejection. With enough setbacks (and poor explanations of them) something happens that is worse than feeling discouraged. The accumulating failures drain away your motivation. Get disheartened enough and your goal starts to seem *undesirable*.

Even if you know how to motivate yourself, you're sunk if you don't know how to undemoralize yourself. Why? Because you can be so thoroughly demoralized that you lose your desire to even try to motivate yourself, making your ability to motivate yourself essentially worthless.

Thinking up goals is easy. Ideas about what you want come easily to mind — maybe too easily. And feeling motivated to take action (to accomplish a goal you want) comes naturally to most people. You want your goal to happen, so of course you're motivated.

But if setting goals is easy and motivation comes naturally, why don't you accomplish every goal you set? Because setbacks demoralize you if you don't explain them well.

It happened to the clergyman. One day, while he was talking to his wife, he decided he had experienced one setback too many. His goal to get his book published became *undesirable*. He threw his manuscript in the trash, saying he'd had enough.

Remember this, please: When you make mistakes in your explanations, it not only nudges you toward failure and giving up and depression, it leads to selling out.

The clergyman's wife knew how much the manuscript meant to him, so she reached into the trash can to pull it out. "No," he said, "I've wasted enough time on it. I forbid you to take it out of there." And she never did.

But the next day, she was thinking about it and got an idea. She took the manuscript — still inside the wastebasket — to another publisher. The publisher, intrigued by this unusual way to bring in a manuscript, read it and loved it. He published it, and boy is he glad he did! The book became one of the bestselling books of all time!

The irony is that the book is *The Power of Positive Thinking* by Norman Vincent Peale.

The story seemed too ironic to be true, so I wrote to the Peales and asked if it was really true. I heard back from Mrs. Peale, who said yes, that's the way it happened.

Positive thinking is different than finding mistakes in your explanations. With positive thinking, I'm sure Dr. Peale would have felt good about throwing that manuscript in the trash. He would have kept his cheerful disposition.

But with mostly mistake-free explanations of setbacks, he would have simply tried again, perhaps in a different way.

We're talking about the ability to try again after a setback — the ability to encounter a setback without giving up in defeat or feeling the goal is hopeless.

What kind of hopeless explanation would make someone throw away their life's work? Dr. Peale must have thought something like, "My book is unpublishable." Or "Nobody wants it."

Mrs. Peale must have explained it differently. Perhaps, "It hasn't been seen by the right publisher." Or maybe even, "It hasn't been delivered the right way yet. Perhaps in a trash can would get someone's attention!"

Explanations matter!

# DEFEATISM IS DEFEATABLE

The one kind of explanation most likely to make you want to give up is an assumption that no matter what you do, you cannot win. This is defeatism. It means you expect defeat. It means you accept defeat and decide there is nothing you can do to change things.

That kind of thinking takes the fight out of you, and if you ever had a chance to change things, it is now lost — only because of what happened in your mind.

But from now on, you will know how to prevent defeatism from destroying your determination. You will have the know-how to find it where it lurks in your mind, and crush it before it causes you to give up.

Defeatist thinking means you assume you can't improve the situation. It is almost always an assumption; rarely a fact. And when you use the antivirus for your mind, you're not replacing that assumption with another assumption. This is not an effort to convince yourself of a positive thought. You are merely leaving the question where it really is: You don't know. When you truly don't know, it is foolish to assume you are helpless. It is unnecessary and self-defeating to decide something cannot be done.

During the Civil War, the situation seemed hopeless several times to the North, even though, of course, the North eventually won. But if you were reading the newspapers of the day, written by Northerners and published in Union newspapers, you might easily believe there was no possible way the North would win. Lots of writers who ardently and desperately *wanted* the North to win nevertheless expressed their absolute certainty of losing. They were demoralized.

For example, an ardent Northern patriot, Joseph Medill of the Chicago Tribune, wrote, "We have to fight for a boundary — that is all now left to us." In other words, winning the Civil War against the South was a lost cause. All that the North could hope for was to draw a boundary and let the Southerners form their own separate government.

"I can understand the awful reluctance with which you can be brought to contemplate a divided nation. But there is no help for it," Medill wrote, "...complete success has become a moral impossibility."

Medill's demoralization was not his alone. During several trying periods, it was shared by a *majority* of people in the North. So many setbacks (combined with the explanations people made of those setbacks) had most Northerners convinced the war could not be won by the North.

Their certainty was premature, as we now know. Their pessimism was overdone, as it usually is.

When Admiral Byrd was a boy in the wrestling match, he assumed he would lose, and he gave up. But what brought him back to life was his realization *he might be mistaken* about that.

If he went a step further and assumed he could win, that would have been positive thinking, which has its place. But anti-defeatism is more sure and more basic, it doesn't require trying to convince yourself of something you are not convinced of, and always should be your first step.

The reality is, people often give up on something and decide it can't be accomplished when it really can. They assume the situation is hopeless when it actually isn't. And so dreams go unfulfilled. Goals are forgotten. Relationships fall apart. Finances crumble. Kids are left without guidance. And so on.

The things you have in your heart — the things *you really want to accomplish* — can probably be accomplished. But you have to prevent your mind from reacting to setbacks by assuming success is hopeless.

The making of a defeatist assumption is almost always *reflexive*, meaning you don't make it consciously. Here's how it happens: You hit a setback and you feel like you've been kicked in the gut. In self-defense, your mind concludes the goal is impossible. It's a natural reaction, almost a reflex. That's defeatism. And the assumptions behind it are almost always wrong.

If a goal is sufficiently important to you, a setback will certainly make you feel bad, no matter who you are or how many times you've read this book. But the way you explain the setback to yourself will then bring you back quickly and help you recover from the blow, or it will keep you feeling bad — or even make you feel worse and worse.

In other words, the way you explain the setback to yourself will determine how quickly your determination comes back, and if it comes back at all.

How do you keep from giving up? How do you keep from selling out? How do you keep from letting your feeling of motivation fade? This is a question for the ages. And now you know the answer.

This applies to any goal you have. If your marriage is on the rocks, the way you're explaining this setback will determine whether you've reached an important turning point in your relationship — or the beginning of the end.

People who make good explanations of setbacks are more likely to exercise and less likely to smoke. Why? Because they are more persistent. They are less likely to feel defeated so they are less likely to give up on what they want. The way they explain setbacks gives them a sense that their actions make a difference — which is a fact that poor explanations conceal. Good explanations prevent them from making the mistake of deciding that something (like a smoking habit) cannot be changed.

If something is *changeable* or *preventable*, it makes a big difference whether you believe it is or believe it isn't.

For example, if you have frequent, negative shouting matches with your teenager, this is a setback. Things are not turning out like you want. So you will explain it. Let's say you decide, "That's just the way teenagers are."

Is that a good explanation? Well, it's better than, "I can't make anything work," but no, it is not a good explanation. Why? Because it implies that the situation can't change until your kid is an adult. And that may not be true. It is a way of "accepting" the situation without feeling too bad about it. But it doesn't help you accomplish your goal — having a good relationship with your teen.

Your explanations determine whether you will try again or not. Making a mistaken explanation like, "That's the way teens are," can kill your motivation to try again.

Sales is a good testing ground for this stuff. Salespeople hit lots of setbacks, and the setbacks are important — too many setbacks and you can't pay your mortgage! That's serious.

MetLife Insurance Company used to hire five thousand salespeople a year, spend time and money training them, and by the end of the first year, half of them quit. Most of those who didn't quit sold less and less, and by the fourth year, eighty percent of them had quit. This was typical of the entire insurance-sales industry, and it was a tragic waste of training expenses and a tragedy of human failure and suffering.

MetLife wanted to do something about it. The cognitive researcher, Martin Seligman, set up a series of experiments and here's what he found out: Those who made the fewest mistakes in their thinking (when they explained their setbacks to themselves) were the most likely to do well. They made a lot more sales and they were much less likely to become demoralized and quit.

Think about that. In a job full of setbacks, strong explanations won the race by a mile. The salespeople in the habit of explaining setbacks with minimum mis-

takes were more successful and less demoralized —
they did better and they felt better.

Good explanations did more than simply make
them persistent. When a salesperson makes fewer mistakes in her explanations, she stops feeling so disheartened by setbacks. So setbacks themselves become less
of a big deal. She then frets less about upcoming sales
presentations. If a sales call doesn't turn out well, she
now knows it won't be a catastrophe. So she has less
anxiety before a sales call, and less demoralization after
a rejection. This makes it easier to make the next call,
which makes success more likely. Her motivation can
remain high because her fire is not being dampened by
feelings of discouragement.

And this is why in all the large-scale, long-term,
carefully controlled experiments, researchers have discovered that people who make relatively mistake-free
explanations of setbacks are more successful at just
about everything than those who don't.

Studies have shown that politicians who make the
best explanations for setbacks *win more elections*, students
who make the best explanations for setbacks *get better
grades*, athletes who make the best explanations *win more
contests*, and salespeople with the best explanations *make
more money*.


## a case in point

To see how the antivirus for the mind works on a
specific problem, a team of researchers took thirty-

three people with panic disorder who averaged five panic attacks per week per person.

Sixteen of them had weekly sessions with a therapist who provided *emotional* support. Seventeen of them had weekly sessions with a cognitive therapist who taught them to check their explanations for mistakes.

For instance, when a man felt chest pain, he was taught to question his explanations. His first explanation of chest pain might be, "I am having a heart attack." And that thought basically scared him into a panic attack. This is a common side-effect of negative thoughts: A self-feeding loop. In other words, a negative thought creates a negative emotion, and the negative emotion causes more negative thoughts, which produces even more intense negative emotions.

In the man's case, a feeling in his chest scared him (because of his explanation of it) and so his heart beat faster, which he could feel, which scared him even more, etc.

The man's cognitive therapist coached him to question his explanation and remind himself that when these feelings occurred in the past, they had never amounted to anything — he never had a heart attack before.

He was also coached to come up with more likely causes than the first thought that came to mind. It was more likely to be heartburn, for example, than a heart attack.

In other words, he learned to doubt his automatic, habitual, negative assumptions. He learned to recognize the mistakes in his thinking. He learned that his first explanation is not the only one possible and not necessarily the best one.

At the end of two months, twelve of the cognitive-therapy people (the explanation-checkers) were totally free of panic attacks. Only four of the emotionally-supported people were free of attacks.

Among those who were still having panic attacks, the explanation-check people averaged one attack a week. The emotional-support people averaged three per week.

The researchers did a one-year follow-up. The success rate did not diminish in that time.

Arguing with their own negative, pessimistic explanations dramatically changed their lives.

Hundreds of similar studies show the same results on a huge variety of negative feelings.

Similar effects to cognitive therapy can be achieved on your own using paper and pen. As a matter of fact, that's often the most effective technique cognitive therapists assign as "homework." It is not difficult to do.

# THE BASIC TECHNIQUE

The next time you feel a negative emotion, get two pens of different color, like red and black. In red, write a negative thought you have about the situation. For example, Harold writes, "Nobody loves me." Someone was rude to Harold, and he still feels bad about it because of his thought, "Nobody loves me."

Now using the black pen, Harold *argues* with his statement. He imagines his least favorite person (his worst enemy) told him, "Nobody loves you."

Once the statement is outside his head, it becomes more objective (and less subjective) so it becomes easier to argue with. When it is *inside* his head, part of him, something he thinks, it's harder to recognize it as mistaken.

Harold takes some time staring at his written statement (nobody loves me) and tries to find something wrong with it. What can he say to that statement? How could he argue with it? Why is it a stupid thing to think? What is mistaken about it?

When you do this, you force the statement to stand trial. Really all of your thoughts ought to get this kind of scrutiny. Nobody really has time for that, but when your thoughts are handicapping you (demoralizing you, making you feel upset, etc.) it is well worth your time.

So he stares at his statement and eventually writes, "That's really not true. I can think of at least two people who love me for sure."

That's pretty good. Harold has found a mistake. Good for him. Do you see how that is different than trying to look on the bright side or repeating to himself, "I am loved I am loved I am loved?" Introducing legitimate doubt about a negative statement has far more emotional impact, and the impact is instantaneous.

So he discovered his first mistake: His negative thought isn't really true. Excellent.

But he shouldn't stop there. He should come up with as many arguments as he can against his statement. He might write, "Maybe there is something I could do — some action I could take — that would make me more lovable. Being loved isn't all-or-nothing anyway." And so on.

The method is simple: Write down something you think about the situation (something negative you believe about the situation) and then try to find something wrong with your statement.

This is an effective way to change how you think about something. It's kind of fun too, once you get going. And you can feel the negative emotion dissipate as you destroy the validity of the pessimistic assumptions that have been ruining your attitude.

Let me remind you that your arguments must be *real*. You're not just playing the "devil's advocate" here. Really look at the statement and find what is truly wrong with it. This is not glossing things over with nice thoughts.

Something many writers on positive thinking don't make clear is that negative thinking is not just counter-productive; it is often objectively wrong. The negative thoughts are *incorrect*. They are exaggerations, over-statements, conclusions you have jumped to, rumors you've heard, or merely bad habits of thinking you randomly formed while growing up.

Your goal with the exercise is to scrutinize your own written statements long enough to discover if there is anything wrong with them. As Carl Sagan said, "Skeptical scrutiny is the means, in both science and religion, by which deep thoughts can be winnowed from deep nonsense."

You might have deep nonsense in one area but not another. You might make good explanations for set-backs in your marriage but make lousy explanations for setbacks at work. The place where this antivirus of the mind is most useful is where you're having difficulties.

Are you having a hard time losing weight? Quitting smoking? Getting in shape? Advancing your career? Feeling close to your kids? Where do you feel defeat-ed? Where have you given up on a goal? Get out your two pens and get to work.

When you feel thwarted or frustrated, check your explanations of setbacks. When you feel like giving up on a goal of yours, check your explanations. If you ever decide to do something and then later feel disappointed in yourself because you didn't follow through, that is a time where checking for mistakes in your explanations will make a huge difference. Pull out those two pens.

Working with the pens like this is not difficult. It is easy to be negative about negative thoughts — far easier than being positive — because you're feeling negative emotions already.

Writing your explanations and arguments with two colored pens is one way. Another is to write out *everything* you think about what's bothering you. And then go back and argue with each sentence one at a time. This is a good variation to use on a computer. Type out every negative thought you have about the situation. And then go back and separate out a sentence and scrutinize it in a different font. Then take the next sentence and search for mistakes in that one. And so on.

Take your whole argument and print it out. Carry it around in your pocket for a few weeks. Re-read it a couple of times a day for even more reinforcement and faster change.

## trying even harder

If someone is in the habit of explaining setbacks poorly (with lots of mistakes), she will experience frequent feelings of demoralization — and she will often give up on her goal, starting projects but not sticking with them, deciding they were foolish goals anyway, and wondering why she came up with them in the first place.

On the other extreme, with a habit of making sensible explanations of setbacks, the same setbacks might make her feel even more determined than before. But how can *setbacks* make someone *more* determined?

In my book, *Self-Help Stuff That Works*, I mention a study done on the Berkeley swim team. The researchers timed each athlete as they swam a familiar distance. At the end of the "timed heat," the coach told them a slower time than they really swam (in order to give them a setback).

They were all experienced competitors and they knew how their swim felt and what their time should be, so it was a small failure to discover they didn't swim as fast as they thought they did.

After the setback, the athletes swam another heat. Prior to all of this swimming, the researchers gave the athletes a test to find out how each one usually explained setbacks to themselves.

Here's the interesting thing: Those who made mistakes in their explanations *felt defeated* after the setback and *swam their next heat slower*. Those with few or no mistakes in their explanations swam their next heat *faster*. They actually tried *harder* after a "defeat."

Why would someone try harder after a setback? For the same reason you would try harder if you played tennis with someone you knew you could beat and your opponent scored a couple points in a row. You'd get *riled up* rather than feeling defeated. Your opponent's scores would focus you and increase your determination to win.

For Norman Vincent Peale, his manuscript was rejected by a long string of publishers. One possible explanation is *nobody wants it*. Can you see how that takes away determination and motivation? It's a thought-mistake. Has he tried *everybody?* No? Then he can't reasonably say "nobody" wants it. It's an overgeneralization. A more sensible explanation might be *I haven't found the right publisher yet*. Notice with *this* explanation (same setback, different explanation) it might make him want to try even *harder*. It might *increase* his determination and motivation.

If you try to talk to your teenager and he is distant and resentful, one possible way to explain that setback is *that's just the way teenagers are*. That is a thought-mistake (overconfidence in a mere guess) and it reduces determination. A more reasonable explanation is *I have not yet found the right approach*. And notice again, this explanation could easily make you want to try *harder*, increasing determination.

A swimmer has a time slower than it should be. One swimmer might think to himself, *I'm past my prime; I'm losing my edge*. Can you feel how that would just suck the life right out of him? Contrast that with an explanation such as, *I didn't get enough sleep last night*. You can't do anything about being "past your prime." But you *can* get more sleep.

I knew a woman who had two failed marriages. Her explanation was *all men are pigs*. Very demoralizing. With a belief like that, would she feel motivated to date again? No, and she didn't. But what about an explanation like this: *My strategy for choosing men needs improvement.* Do you see how dramatically different that explanation is? Can you imagine what different results she might get with it?

Or how about a man who has had a heart attack. One way to explain that is *I'm destined to die young.* With an explanation like that, would the man change his diet? Change his attitude? Improve his marriage? Probably not. He would be too demoralized to do anything. Compare that with an explanation like this: *Up until now, I haven't been motivated to take good care of my health.* Do you see how that leaves room for change? How it *motivates?* How it doesn't at all demoralize?

And I know this is being repetitive, but I need to hammer on this: The second explanation has a better *result*, but it is also *truer.* Do not, I repeat: DO NOT just try to come up with a "positive" explanation. If you don't really believe it, your new improved explanation won't help you one little bit.

A salesman has ten people in a row say no. One explanation is, *I'm the worst salesman who ever lived.* Not very inspiring. Not likely to help get the next prospect to say yes. As opposed to *I need to learn more about sales.* Or even the typical sales principle, *this is a numbers game. It's just the odds. If I keep trying, I'll get someone to say yes.* It's a better explanation because it is *truer* and gives you a better result.

I once wanted to speak in public but even the thought of it made me nervous. My explanation of my nervousness was *I am constitutionally shy; my fear proves I can't do it.* That is full of thought-mistakes (overgeneralization, false permanence, mistaken unchangeability, extremism — you'll learn about these a little later in this book). A more reasonable explanation that did in fact make me want to try harder was it *is normal to feel nervous; it is merely a lack of experience.* It made me want to get more experience speaking. As soon as I started using this new explanation, my feelings about speaking changed surprisingly quickly.

# YOUR FEELINGS
# WILL CHANGE QUICKLY

The best news about the antivirus for your mind is that the moment you recognize that one of your negative thoughts is nonsense, the spell is broken. Immediately. You don't have to wait for some vague reward in the future.

If you think, "I'm helpless to do anything about it," and you really look at that assumption and find you have very little evidence to justify such a sweeping allegation, your negative feelings evaporate. As soon as you recognize you have been mistaken, your demoralization vanishes, literally within minutes.

Your feelings are influenced by your thoughts, but *only* the thoughts you truly *believe*. If you don't believe it, a thought will have zero impact on your feelings. That's why positive thinking sometimes doesn't work. But it's also why as soon as you find something wrong with a pessimistic thought — the moment you realize you were mistaken and you stop believing it — your feelings change.

It's not what you say to yourself that makes a difference. It's what you *believe*. And not what you can "get yourself" to believe, but what you really and truly think is true.

When you think, "Dustin is a jerk," and you feel angry because of it, as soon as you recognize it's merely a label and therefore (by definition) an over-statement, your feeling of anger diminishes. Immed-iately. You now don't believe Dustin is a jerk. Maybe you think he doesn't speak very nicely to you some-times for reasons you don't know, but that's more in line with reality and not as angering.

Your new, more reasonable explanation makes you realize that you don't speak nicely sometimes and other people occasionally don't know why. We are all just human. That doesn't mean you have to love Dustin, or even like him. Remember, this is not trying to do any-thing positive. Just take the negative nonsense out of your explanations.

If you find one of your demoralizing explanations is true, okay. Leave it alone. Don't try to gloss it over with niceness just because it makes you feel bad. Sometimes you will feel bad, because sometimes reality sucks. But more times than not, the explanations mak-ing you sad or angry or worried *are wrong*. They contain mistakes.

Often something that was a big problem fizzles away into nothing under the glaring scrutiny of your earnest search for thought-mistakes. You will find a few mistakes in your thinking, you will see through the illusion, and *poof* — the problem disappears. Not always, but it happens.


## trigger the explanation-check

So the good news is that your feelings change quickly. The bad news is: Even though you know this, and even though you don't like feeling bad, you will still forget to use it. At the time you're feeling bad, it probably won't occur to you to do anything about it. Bad feelings have a kind of mesmerizing, hypnotic effect. Bad feelings capture your attention — making you forget things you already know.

So you need to make setbacks *trigger* an explanation-check. Associate setbacks (and the feeling of demoralization that follows) with an explanation-check. Associate it so many times, it becomes an automatic habit with you to check your explanations *every* time a setback happens. Whenever you feel bad, you want it to *occur to you* that you can do something about it.

You're reading this chapter and thinking this sounds like a great idea, and you can't wait to feel bad so you can try it (wink). A week from now you'll realize you haven't caught yourself even *once*. Setbacks have happened, you explained them to yourself automatically and without even knowing you were doing it, and you went right on feeling bad but never reflecting on the fact that you had any choice in the matter. Then later you'll look back and think, "Oh yeah, I was supposed to check my explanations."

But if you keep trying, you can do it. Do you believe me? If you don't, or if you try and fail, then make sure you check your explanations for that setback!

Keep trying. Make this something you focus on for the next few months. Have a necklace made for yourself that says, "Check explanations every setback" and wear it around your neck. Write it on a card and carry it in your pocket. Put it on the screensaver of your computer.

And I don't mean do *one* of these things. I mean do *all* of these things and anything else you can think of. This is very serious business. The way you explain setbacks determines to a large extent how your life will turn out! The way you explain setbacks to yourself has an impact on everything important to you. It affects your ability to succeed, it affects your ability to solve problems, it affects your relationships, and it affects your health.

Forming the habit of checking your explanations can significantly change the rest of your life. This is not something to be half-assed about.

Make some signs that say, "Check explanations every setback" and post them on your bathroom mirror, on the dashboard of your car, on the refrigerator door. Put one in your closet where you'll see it every morning. Tell your son to remind you of it every morning and you'll give him a dollar for reminding you. And try try try. You will fail a lot. Each time you realize you've gone the whole day and didn't once catch yourself explaining a setback, that *itself* is a setback, so check right then how you're explaining it!

*Every* time you feel bad, write down what you're thinking and argue with it. That's how you form the habit.

A sluggish computer probably makes you think, "It's time to run a virus scan (to search for and remove viruses and malware from your computer)." In the same way, a negative emotion should automatically make you think it's time to search for and disabuse yourself of mistaken negative thoughts.

What is the *first* thing to do when you feel a negative emotion? (I'm quizzing you now.) Answer: Clean your mind of mistaken explanations of setbacks. Do a virus scan of your brain.

You don't really need to know anything more about the antivirus for the mind. With what you've learned so far, you can very effectively change your feelings and accomplish your goals with more certainty. But a few more pieces of information can make it easier.

# VIRUS DEFINITIONS

The basic principle is to argue with your negative thoughts. On paper is better than in your head. How do you argue with your thoughts? Write one down, imagine your worst enemy said it, and then argue with it.

When you're arguing with your statements, it helps to have specific things to look for — specific mistakes in your negative thoughts. It makes your task easier to work from a list and check your statements against the list. This is the way a computer's antivirus program works.

With most antivirus programs, you are constantly getting updates, which are "definitions" of new viruses. As new viruses are created, the antivirus people make a definition of it. Then the antivirus program scans your computer looking for those specific definitions — basically checking the content of your computer against its list of virus definitions.

What if you could do something similar with your mind? What if you had a list of "virus definitions" and all you had to do was scan your thoughts looking for them?

Cognitive scientists have made several such lists. They are all fairly similar and cover the same ground because the human brain only makes mistakes in certain specific, definable ways. So your virus definition list doesn't need to be constantly updated.

Shortly I will give you a list of the finite number of common mistakes people make when they explain setbacks.

With this list you can search through your own negative thoughts and see if you're making any of the mistakes. To see clearly what you're trying to do, let's imagine you're searching through someone else's negative thoughts and finding mistakes in them.

Imagine you receive a letter from a good friend. He is on vacation and you haven't seen him in a month. But in his letter, he has clearly had some sort of crisis. He is despairing and upset. One of the paragraphs of his letter goes like this:

> I realized nobody really cares about me and
> I've never done a good thing in my whole life.
> I have problems I can't do anything about.
> Nothing I do will make any difference.

Let's say you cannot call him because he's in the Australian outback or something. You have to *write* him back. What would you say? You would want to straighten him out on a few things, wouldn't you? First of all, you know of at least one person who really cares about him: *You*. You'd want to point out his exaggerations and overstatements and tell him his point of view is only narrow because he is upset right now. He's not seeing the whole picture. He's ignoring some genuine positives in his life.

You may try to do it nicely, but you will try very hard to point out that *some of his thoughts are mistaken.*

When you are cleaning out your own mind when you feel bad, you are essentially doing the same thing. You're finding mistakes in your negative thinking — mistakes that make you feel worse than is really just-ified by the facts. When you look at a negative thought and realize it is mistaken, you'll feel better — instantly.

Imagine another situation. You have two kids and a spouse. You are always telling them to lock the door when they leave the house. Today you come home from work to find nobody home and the house un-locked. You start to get mad, thinking about what you're going to say to your young miscreants when you suddenly realize *you* were the last one to leave the house, and *you* forgot to lock it.

Do you realize how fast your emotions would change? The *instant* you realized you were mistaken, your feelings would switch. The anger would change to embarrassment or even laughter. Instantly.

The same goes with your thought-mistakes. The second you recognize one of your thoughts was mis-taken, your emotions change.

When you write down your negative thoughts and stare at them and can't find anything wrong with them, check them against these thought-mistakes. Sometimes it is not obvious what is mistaken about your negative thoughts. That's what the list is for.

You don't have to memorize the list. Right now just read through the descriptions to get a good idea of all the different ways the human brain (and its natural way of working) makes mistakes. Here's the list. Descriptions will follow:

1. exaggerating
2. overgeneralizing
3. oversimplifying
4. extremism
5. overcertainty
6. negative guessing
7. self-defeating conclusions
8. false implications
9. choosing the worst possible explanation
10. false helplessness
11. false hopelessness
12. shoulds and musts
13. misplacing responsibility
14. focusing too narrowly
15. harmful judging
16. asking unanswerable questions
17. bias for confirmation
18. using emotions as evidence
19. dismissing facts
20. ignoring alternatives
21. assuming
22. negative bias

Let's take these one at a time and define them.

# 1. exaggerating

"WHEN I WAS DRIVING to work today, the other drivers were all so *aggressive*," says Karen, who looks quite harassed. When asked about details it turns out only *two* drivers acted aggressively. Two drivers out of the hundreds she shared the roads with.

This is one of the most typical thought-mistakes, and you can see why it would make Karen feel unnecessary negative emotions. Two out of hundreds of drivers acting aggressively is really saying hundreds of people did *not* act aggressively and that's not really something to get upset about.

But "everyone is so aggressive" can easily be an upsetting thought.

When I first started writing for publication, I would ask my wife, Klassy, to edit for me, and the most common thing she wanted to change was my propensity for overstating my case. I was young and I had never thought about that before. But she would often scratch out a sentence like, "This method will work every time," and put in something like, "It works most of the time." And her revisions were not only more true, but they were more *believable*. I was overstating my case and losing the credibility of my readers in the process.

It can be misleading in writing and it can be misleading when you think it in your head. Exaggerated negative thoughts make you feel exaggerated negative emotions. As soon as you recognize that one of your thoughts is an exaggeration, your negative emotions calm down quickly.

## 2. overgeneralizing

THIS IS ONE OF the most common thought-mistakes. It is necessary to generalize — to see patterns that help you make your way through the world — but *overgeneralization* can make you feel miserable unnecessarily.

Because of the way our brains function, we tend to make certain kinds of mistakes. These are naturally-occurring mistakes, the kind of errors *every* brain is prone to make. In a way, the "mistakes" are simply side-effects of a well-functioning, incredibly capable brain.

Researchers at Duke University Medical Center hooked people up to a high-resolution functional MRI machine (to track the blood flow in the brain) and flashed pictures in front of them. The pictures were of either a square or a circle. They were asked to push the button in their *right* hand when they saw a square, and push the button in their *left* hand for a circle.

The squares and circles were presented in a random order, but of course short patterns would sometimes emerge — a string of all squares, for example, or an alternation between a square and a circle for several cycles.

Their brains reacted with extra blood flow when one of these short patterns ended. In other words, their brains automatically detected and generalized patterns, and very quickly. They were given no reward for detecting patterns. They were not asked to detect patterns. In fact, they were told the pictures would be flashed randomly. Yet even so, without any effort on their part, their brains automatically saw patterns in the random events and *generalized* — they began to anticipate what the next picture would be.

In previous similar studies testing their reaction time, the volunteers had a slower reaction time when an expected pattern was broken.

Your brain is predisposed to generalize. It automatically tries to see patterns without any conscious participation or effort on your part.

By and large, our ability to generalize is a good thing. For example, Ignaz Semmelweis noticed when doctors performed a dissection and then assisted in a birth, the women had a tendency to get childbed fever. He was able to detect a *pattern*, to make a generalization, and it led to the practice of using antiseptics and sterilization, saving *millions* of unnecessary deaths over time.

Charles Darwin saw a pattern that governs the evolution of all life on earth. From that single generalization, new understandings about diseases were discovered that greatly improved the effectiveness of doctors. In fact, whole new sciences have issued from that single generalization.

What I'm trying to say is: The mistakes our brains tend to make (like overgeneralizing) are the inevitable byproducts of our great intelligence.

Your ability to recognize a face comes from your brain's ability to complete a pattern with minimal clues.

It was exceedingly difficult to create computer software that could do it.

Your brain recognizes faces without any effort on your part. Your brain is so good at completing a pattern that, even in dim light — even if you can only see half of the face — you recognize immediately who it is.

But this amazing ability also sometimes causes us to see patterns that don't really exist. We see a man in the moon. We see a horse in the clouds. We see the big dipper, the little dipper, Orion's belt. Our brains can take the most scant clues and see a pattern, without us making even the smallest effort to do so.

But especially given our brains' bias toward negativity (see virus definition number 22), we also see patterns that create pessimism, cynicism, and defeatism — patterns our brains have created out of minimal clues — patterns *that don't actually exist.*

The woman I used to work with (who had two failed marriages) concluded, "All men are pigs." From only two examples, she created a generalization that judged *billions* of men! Her cynicism, her unwillingness to allow any men to get close to her, was the side-effect of two common mistakes our brains tend to make: 1) the brain's amazing ability to see a pattern with minimal clues, and 2) our brain's tendency to look for evidence that confirms an already-existing conclusion.

In other words, your brain tends to overgeneralize and then the world seems to prove you're right about it.

The two primary mistakes that turn generalizations into overgeneralizations are:

**1. Holding the generalization as a fact rather than an hypothesis.** Any generalization you make is a *guess*. You will have some degree of certainty about your guess — you can be quite certain your guess is correct, you can be very uncertain about your guess, or anywhere in between. When you have more certainty about your generalization than the facts justify, it is an overgeneralization. You've gone too far.

**2. Generalizing from too few instances.** Researchers have discovered that people don't have a very accurate sense of what "chance sequences" look like. People expect sequences of coin flips, for example, to alternate more than they actually do. So truly random sequences can often *look* like a pattern to us.

In a series of twenty coin tosses, you have a fifty-fifty chance of getting four heads in a row; you have a twenty-five percent chance of getting five in a row; you have a ten percent chance of getting six in a row! And yet we sometimes predict a pattern from only one or two incidents — a person has two mishaps in one afternoon and concludes, "Everything is going wrong today." That's an overgeneralization, and it causes unnecessary suffering.

Everybody makes these kinds of mistakes at least some of the time. Even the experts. Our brains are so ready and willing to generalize, it's inevitable we're going to go overboard now and then and overgeneralize. Here are a few historical examples:

- Marshal Foch, a competent, well-informed military leader, said in 1911, "Airplanes are interesting toys, but they have no military value."

- On October 16th, 1929, the economist Irving Fisher said, "Stocks have reached what looks like a permanently high plateau." The stock market crash that started the Great Depression began two weeks later.

- "Whatever happens," said Frank Knox, U.S. Secretary of the Navy, "the U.S. Navy is not going to be caught napping." He said this on December 4, 1941. The Japanese bombed Pearl Harbor three days later.

- In 1958, Business Week printed this: "With over 50 foreign cars already on sale here, the Japanese auto industry isn't likely to carve out a big slice of the U.S. market."

These were experts in their field, stating their opinions with *too much confidence*. It's a common human error. From now on and for the rest of your life, be suspicious of your feelings of certainty — about your overgeneralizations or about any explanations of setbacks. You will save yourself untold amounts of suffering.

In the book, *Dying of Embarrassment*, I found an interesting piece of information. People with a social phobia — people who find it very difficult to tolerate dealing with a social situation — make two particular kinds of assumptions. They assume they are *very* likely to meet disapproval in the social situation, and they assume that the *consequences* of that disapproval will be really bad. But their assumptions are exaggerated. Their predictions are mistaken. Their projections of the future are distorted. They exaggerate the "social danger."

They exaggerate the threat, probably because they explained past social setbacks with exaggerations. So now they make what are called "probability distortions" and "severity distortions" and these make them far more uptight and nervous than the reality of the situation merits or deserves.

To *assume* something is going to turn out badly is putting too much confidence in a guess — a guess that makes you ineffective and unhappy.

After a shipwreck, when someone says, "We're not going to make it," that thought is wrong because there is still a chance they'll make it, so there's no justification for certainty about doom. It's even more of a mistake because they are less likely to *survive* thinking that way.

When using the antivirus for your mind, you will often realize you don't know. That's *okay*. In fact, finding yourself with greater uncertainty is *good*. When you don't know, your mind is open. If you decide you know and you're wrong, you shut your mind to what's really going on.

When you scan your thoughts looking for "mind viruses," overgeneralizations should be one of the first things you look for.


## permanence

The researcher Martin Seligman and his colleagues have discovered that the most deadly assumption you can make about the cause of a setback is: *The cause is permanent*, meaning that you can't do anything about it and it isn't going to change on its own either. Permanence is almost always an overgeneralization — and a dangerous one if it isn't true.

Whether you think of something as temporary or permanent changes your feelings drastically. I remember once Klassy and I were ready for four days of total peace and quiet at a resort on the Pacific coast. The first morning we were awakened at 7:30 AM by what sounded like a hundred people laughing and stomping around in the hotel room above us.

We were both bothered by this. We went down to the office and said, "The people above us are making lots of noise."

"What unit number are you in?" asked the woman at the desk.

"Number nine."

"Well, if it makes you feel any better, that party is leaving today. Checkout time is noon. And the room is not rented for the next few days." We went back to the room and the noises were still there but they didn't bother us any more.

Why? Because it was *temporary*.

Permanence says, "This is always going to be here," or "there's no way out of it." It evokes feelings of *demoralization*. It makes you want to give up. That's not a helpful response to a setback.

Interestingly, one of the things Napoleon Hill hammers on in his books (*The Law of Success, Think and Grow Rich*, and *Success Through A Positive Mental Attitude*) is that failure is only "temporary defeat."

Hill and Seligman are trying to get their readers to do the same thing: Avoid jumping to the conclusion that this setback is *permanent*. It's a deadly assumption. It stops action. It kills motivation. It destroys dreams. Don't ever do it again!

Napoleon Hill was commissioned by the richest man in the world at the time — Andrew Carnegie — to write a philosophy of success. Carnegie thought it was a shame that each person had to figure out what it takes to succeed by trial and error, only to have that accumulated know-how die with them. He thought it should be written down. Carnegie asked Hill to do it.

So Napoleon Hill interviewed the most famous successful people of his day: Thomas Edison, Henry Ford, William Wrigley, Jr., George Eastman — over five hundred of them. He discovered how they succeeded and shared his findings in his books.

Hill became famous too, and very well-respected. President Woodrow Wilson put Hill on his staff as an advisor during World War I. And Hill served as an advisor to President Franklin D. Roosevelt throughout most of the Great Depression. It was Napoleon Hill who came up with Roosevelt's famous saying, "We have nothing to fear but fear itself."

In all his books, the principle Hill seemed to emphasize more than any other was: Think of a "failure" as merely "temporary defeat." Or, as Seligman might put it: If the cause of the setback *isn't* permanent, make sure you don't *assume* it is.

If you can restrain yourself from deciding the cause of a setback is permanent, you will be healthier, happier, and more successful. An undiscourageable explanatory style moves you toward accomplishment, success, persistence, courage, and determination. It moves you closer to success and health and happiness.

Researchers like Seligman were studying depression, but what they ended up with is essentially a science of determination.


## overgeneralizing influences memory

When I was first learning to make public presentations, I had more than one embarrassing moment, but I also had many good moments. At first I made an overgeneralization that blocked out the good moments — I said to myself, "I get too nervous." And that thought made me more nervous than I needed to be, creating still more embarrassing moments than I would have had otherwise.

It was an overgeneralization because much of the time (in fact, *most* of the time) I wasn't too nervous.

But by overgeneralizing, I unnecessarily increased my dread of speaking. Overgeneralizing the bad very often makes things worse.

For example, I was once looking for a store in the Yellow Pages (back when they had Yellow Pages!). I used to hate using the Yellow Pages because I "never" seemed to be able to find what I was looking for. This time I wanted to find a mall so I looked under "mall." It said to look under "department stores" or "outlets." I got a headache. Then I realized my thought was, "I always have trouble finding stuff in the Yellow Pages."

The word *always* is a strong indication that you are probably overgeneralizing.

You have to be careful about the "evidence" for your generalizations. Our memories can be skewed merely because some things naturally make more of an impression than others. If I look something up in the Yellow Pages and find it right away, what is there to remember? But if I search and search and get frustrated and throw the phonebook at the wall, it is memorable.

So just because of this difference, if I searched my own memory, I would get the impression that I "usually" have difficulty finding what I want in the Yellow Pages, even if most of the times I looked, I easily found what I was looking for. And it would seem to me I have good *evidence* for my conclusion — I remember plenty of times of frustration and I don't recall many instances where I found something easily, because it wasn't very memorable.

Stressful moments are easier to remember than emotionally-flat moments, and because of that, we can overgeneralize — falsely see a negative pattern that doesn't really exist. It's an illusion caused by the way our brains store and retrieve memories.

An interesting experiment clarifies this point. At the University of California, researchers showed subjects two narrated slide shows. One was a boring account of a boy visiting a hospital and watching the medical staff preparing for a surgical procedure. The other one showed the boy getting run over by a car and getting emergency care.

Before watching the film, half the people were given a beta blocker — a drug that blocks two stress hormones, adrenaline and noradrenaline. The other half were given a pill containing no active ingredients of any kind (a placebo).

A week later, everyone took a test to find out how much of the slide shows they remembered. They all remembered everything equally, except the stressful parts. The ones who got the placebo remembered the traumatic parts of the story with greater clarity than the ones who took the beta blocker.

In other words, *because of the stress hormones*, stressful events are naturally more memorable.

In *Consumer Reports on Health*, they had this to say about the experiment:

Mundane happenings can be difficult to remember. But upsetting events are often hard to forget...A separate, more durable system for storing emotionally charged memories has survival value, the researchers pointed out, enabling animals to remember and avoid threatening situations.

Let's recap for a moment. 1) stressful events are more memorable because they are more dramatic and noticeable — they stick out, 2) the brain itself records stressful events differently so you remember them better, and 3) you see patterns at the drop of a hat — your brain can (and often does) see a pattern where there really isn't one.

These three factors combine into one of the most common sources of bad feelings: Overgeneralizations. When writing this chapter, I was thinking up examples, one after the other, writing them down. Then I started writing one down but I stopped because it was a stupid example. I crumpled it up and thought, "Maybe I'm out of good examples."

See what I did? I overgeneralized from a *single* example of failure. I remember doing that when my first book had just been published and I went around to the local bookstores to ask them to carry it. Most bookstore owners said yes. I went around a few weeks later to see if my book was on their shelves and in one of the major bookstores, it wasn't. The thoughts zipping through my head at the time were, "This is going to be harder than I thought. Maybe I was being naive. Maybe I don't really know anything and I'm just fooling myself." I overgeneralized and felt dejected.

Overgeneralizations are extremely common. (I was going to say "everybody does it all the time" but that is an overgeneralization.) When something bad happens and you say, "It figures," that's a demoralizing overgeneralization. When you say, "That's just my luck," ditto. These presume permanence.

Overgeneralizations are hard to detect because you assume whatever *you* think is true. They would be easy to detect if someone was angry at you and said something like, "You never wash the dishes." You would immediately remember many times when you washed the dishes. But when you say something like that to *yourself*, you don't question it. You just feel bad.


## the grinder people

When I was young, I worked in a restaurant that served Prime Rib sandwiches, which for some reason, in the restaurant business they call "grinders." One day a couple came in and sat in Scott's section (one of the other waiters) and ordered Prime Rib sandwiches.

Scott was very busy that day and didn't give the couple very good service. They tipped him poorly.

Scott decided, based on this single instance, that this couple was "cheap." He overgeneralized. He saw a pattern in a single instance. He talked it up and grumbled about it to everyone who would listen (making his hasty conclusion public and therefore harder to change).

As it turns out, a few days later, the same couple came in and sat in Scott's section again. And again, they ordered two Prime Rib sandwiches.

This time Scott wasn't very busy, but since he already "knew" they weren't going to tip him much, he gave them lousy service, and they proved him right: They tipped him poorly again. This is one of the problems with overgeneralizing about the permanence of a bad event. It can become a self-fulfilling prophesy.

From then on, when that couple came in, no matter whose section they sat in, Scott would go talk to their waiter: "See those two people? Those are the Grinder People I've been telling you about!" And that waiter would then give them careless service, and they tipped badly.

But they kept coming in. They must have really loved those Prime Rib sandwiches!

One day they sat in my section. I had been reading about this stuff and decided to avoid overgeneralizing and gave them great service. And what do you know? They tipped me really well!

After that, they asked for my section when they came in. I served them many times and they always tipped me well.

The tendency to overgeneralize is built into our brains. But there is a cure for it. The cure is simple: *Catch yourself* overgeneralizing. Over and over and over. Keep it up and your tendency will gradually diminish.

You may now realize this would be a great thing to change in your thinking. If you then think, "I'll never follow through on it — I'm not persistent enough with stuff like that," you have your first overgeneralization to question.

## 3. oversimplifying

WHEN YOU USE the antivirus for your mind, you usually don't need to know all the possible thought-mistakes. You can just be reasonable and really look at your statements, and even if you don't know exactly what's wrong, you can tell when something isn't right about your explanations.

But it's worth reading through this list of thought-mistakes and their descriptions. If nothing else, it will give you a clear general idea of what thought-mistakes are.

Oversimplifying is a very broad mistake, and it can show up in many different ways. One way is labeling others. If you meet someone and he seems socially awkward, you may think to yourself, "He's a nerd."

He may be kind to strangers, take care of his mother, have a fascinating hobby, have a rich and varied emotional and intellectual life, but you have made the mistake of oversimplifying by giving him a single label to sum up a single facet of his complex personality. It's not fair and it's not correct and if you make this mistake under certain conditions it can cause depression, anxiety, or anger — unnecessarily.

Al Seibert, the author of *The Survivor Personality*, says "labeling" turns people into nouns, which, he says, is "a child's way of thinking. It limits understanding. It strips away what is unique about an individual and restricts the mind of the beholder to inaccurate generalizations."

Seibert is concerned with what makes a good survivor under difficult circumstances like shipwrecks and POW camps. And his research has shown: "A more effective way to view people, and one that allows better understanding, is to assume that every person is more complex, unpredictable, and unique than any label." Resisting the natural temptation to oversimplify your judgments of others, in other words, can help you survive in dangerous situations.

Another way to oversimplify is to tell someone else *their* motivation. For example, John bought flowers for Jeanne partly because he felt guilty for staying so late at the office, partly because he just loves her and knows she likes flowers, and partly because he enjoys how her mood perks up when she has flowers in a vase sitting on the table. But when she gets the flowers she says, "You're just giving me these because you feel guilty."

Jeanne's statement is an oversimplification, and so to that degree, *it is inaccurate*. But the emotions she feels will be a response to the oversimplification rather than to the real (more complex) situation.

It may be simpler and easier in some ways to oversimplify, but often it makes for bad feelings that are totally unnecessary and unsuitable to the real situation.


## 4. extremism

THIS IS PROBABLY the most dangerous and one of the most common thought-mistakes. Extremism is thinking in black-or-white terms. It's also called "all-or-nothing thinking." The real world has very few absolutes. Very few issues — very few causes of setbacks — are black or white. They consist of innumerable shades of gray.

Becky thinks if she's not a millionaire, she's a failure. Of course, if she's not a millionaire, this belief will make her feel bad unnecessarily. Jeff thinks he must either weigh his ideal weight or he's a fat slob. This kind of all-or-nothing, one-extreme-or-the-other thinking will cause him unnecessary misery whenever he is not at his ideal weight.

Edmund Burke wrote, "Nobody made a greater mistake than he who did nothing because he could only do a little." If you do *nothing* because you can only do a little, that's extremist thinking. Specifically, it is the mistake of all-or-nothing thinking. It makes you defeated unless things are ideal, and since life is almost never ideal, it is a way of thinking that curtails positive action and prevents positive emotions.

Thinking in an extremist way may make it *easier* to think about things. You can separate issues cleanly, and then position yourself on one side or the other, end of story, no more thought required.

But reality is full of shades of gray, so although you've made your task easier, you've greatly increased your chances of being wrong. As a congressman once said on the issue of whiskey:

If you mean the demon drink that poisons the mind, pollutes the body, desecrates family life, and inflames sinners, then I am against it. But if you mean the elixir of Christmas cheer, the shield against winter chill, the taxable potion that puts needed funds into public coffers to comfort little crippled children, then I'm for it. This is my position and I will not compromise.

Almost every issue is like that. But the way our brains are set up, it keeps pulling us to one side or another in an effort to avoid living with the ambiguity. *But reality is often ambiguous.* It would be in your best interest to tolerate that ambiguity, although this is difficult to do. But just because you don't do it perfectly doesn't mean it's not worth doing at all (wink).

Alistair Ostell, a researcher in England, surveyed school principals and tested them for black-or-white thinking. Here's what he found: The principals who frequently thought in black-or-white terms had more emotional problems and more health problems.

The principals who thought more in shades of gray were less stressed by their jobs, enjoyed better health, and got more enjoyment from their work.

*There are real consequences to the accuracy of your thinking.*

Learn to catch yourself making this mistake (extremism) and learn to *recognize* it as a mistake, and you will avoid some negative emotions you don't need.

I once did a speech in Toastmasters (a club that helps you learn to speak in public) on the day before Saint Patrick's Day. The assignment was to give an "inspirational speech." I wrote and memorized a presentation about Saint Patrick, and then rehearsed it thirty-seven times start to finish, flawlessly. (I counted because I wanted to see how many times it took to know a talk by heart.)

A key element of my speech was the *mystery*: The audience wouldn't find out I was talking about Saint Patrick until the end.

But the Toastmaster that day (the Master of Ceremonies), in her opening remarks, told the brief story of Saint Patrick — essentially summarizing my talk before I gave it. That really threw me off.

When I got up to speak, I said, "The Toastmaster gave away my punch line." Then I felt embarrassed I'd criticized her. By then I was really distracted and could not think of the next line of my speech.

It was a crummy speech and I'm sure it was uncomfortable for the audience to endure.

In the Toastmasters meetings, after you have given your speech, an "evaluator" comes up in front of the group to criticize the way you spoke. My evaluator had a lot of negative things to say about my speech.

For someone who had been anxious about speaking, this hit me pretty hard. I went home feeling embarrassed and ashamed of myself, and felt really down about the whole thing.

And you know what that means. You'd *better* know what that means by now! Whenever you feel down, *check your explanations.*

As soon as I got home, I checked my explanations, and I found two thoughts that qualified as irrational. They were the main source of my bad feelings: "I'm not cut out for speaking," and "I'm not an inspirational speaker." Both of these are the mistake of extremist, black-or-white thinking.

After I uncovered those, I came to my senses. I stopped feeling bad and I realized I had simply made a mistake. I should avoid memorizing speeches whenever possible. It just doesn't work as well as other ways of preparing. I also realized that if I ever had an element of mystery in a speech again, I would check with the master of ceremonies to make sure nobody would give away my punch line.

In other words, after realizing that my fretting and negative emotions were being generated by unreasonable thoughts, I stopped fretting and actually solved the problem.

After discovering my two extremist assumptions, I no longer felt depressed about my speech, or demoralized about public speaking in general. My thinking became more rational and more effective — and *quickly* — because I knew what to look for.


## 5. overcertainty

USING THE ANTIVIRUS for your mind, you first write down negative thoughts you have when you feel discouraged. Next, you look at those thoughts, one at a time, to see if they contain mistakes. A common mistake is *overcertainty*.

Look at your negative statement and see whether or not you really have enough evidence to justify your explanation of the setback.

You will often find your "evidence" is rather weak and wouldn't be enough to convince you if you heard someone else say it. Zipping through your mind without examining it, the thought may pass. But write it down and look at it and you may at once have the horrifying realization that you're full of bullpucky.

Ask this question of all *negative* thoughts: Does the evidence *compel* you to accept your conclusion? Please understand me here. The question is not: "do you have some evidence for your conclusion?" But rather, is the evidence so strong that you *must* accept your pessimistic conclusion? That is a much higher standard, and since it is vitally important that you refuse to accept a demoralizing conclusion unless you must (because the consequences are so dangerous), having a high standard is the only sane way to handle negative thoughts.

Standing before a jury, would you be able to convince them that your explanation is the *only* valid one? Or the *best* one? If you were in the jury and heard your argument, would *you* be convinced?

This is the core principle of the scientific method, and the reason science progressively increases our understanding of the world.

Human history can be seen as the progressive realization that we are talking out our asses. In other words, ever since people could speak, they have been saying untrue things with a lot of confidence.

Slowly but surely, we have disabused ourselves of mistaken notions. How? By constantly looking through this filter: Do we have enough evidence to *compel* us to accept this or that notion?

Here's just one example I've come across recently. Native Americans cultivated their environment much more than the first Europeans suspected. When the

Europeans landed on the New England coast, it was obvious that the Native Americans lived in harmony with nature — fishing, hunting, doing a little gardening, but otherwise living the wild life.

Only recently have archaeologists discovered that Native Americans had *created* this wild environment to suit them. They were semi-farming, and doing it in a way that Europeans didn't recognize as farming. It all looked like naturally-occurring abundance, and that's what they all assumed, and they were, of course, quite certain about it.

But that certainty is eroding as new findings come in. Digging through remains, scientists have found evidence of massive and repeated fires. Looking through first-hand reports of Europeans' very first contacts with Native Americans, here and there one of them mentions some of the things Native Americans were doing, such as deliberately burning areas.

Adding all the evidence together, we see an entirely different picture. It was a Native American practice throughout much of the Americas to burn off huge areas of forest. Then they either planted fruit and nut trees, or simply let the grass grow, which brought large grazing animals into the area, which the Native Americans could then hunt.

When Europeans arrived, they saw large areas of grassland filled with game, and incredibly rich forests. It looked like pure luck that the Native Americans could wander into their nearby forests and pick hazelnuts, chestnuts, hickory nuts, beechnuts, acorns, butternuts, pecans, and walnuts. But it wasn't luck at all. The whole area was created deliberately.

They were farming, but not in any familiar way, so it was overlooked. Europeans drew conclusions with too much certainty, as we all do from time to time, and it prevented them from seeing what was really there.

All of us would benefit from paying attention to our own feelings of certainty, and to ask ourselves how sure we really are about what we've concluded.

## 6. negative guessing

WHEN YOU MAKE a guess, it helps to realize it is just a guess, especially when your guess is making you feel defeated, demoralized, or otherwise unhappy. As soon as you realize a particular negative guess is just a guess, it takes the power out of it and you stop feeling bad.

I know a man who is cynical about the president, the governors, and politicians in general. He is glum often because he thinks he knows what they're all after. He's sure they're only interested in money and power and they don't care about "the people."

In other words, he is guessing the motivations of politicians and then he becomes depressed and bitter because of his guess.

It's not uncommon for people to do the same sort of thing, not just about other people, but about future events. "It's not going to work out," you might hear someone say, and she believes her guess, so she does not even try. She is guessing what's going to happen in the future. She's making a negative guess and feeling defeated by it.

Can you see how different it would be to not guess but to merely acknowledge to yourself that you don't know? If that's the truth, *if you really don't know*, just admit it. Not knowing may make you feel an uncomfortable degree of curiosity or frustration, but it won't make you feel demoralized or angry. It won't make you want to give up on a goal. It will not deflate your motivation. It won't ruin your attitude and it won't close your mind.

# 7. self-defeating conclusions

ALMOST ALL THE thought-mistakes on the list of virus definitions are some form of self-defeating conclusions. But this is a good one to look for on its own.

For example, Jim's boss is usually friendly, but today his boss seems unhappy. Jim immediately jumps to a negative conclusion: "I must have done something wrong. He seems mad at me."

Jim's boss is actually worried about his own daughter. The look on the boss's face has nothing to do with Jim. So Jim is feeling unnecessarily anxious because of his thought-mistake. And his bad feelings might interfere with his work. It certainly doesn't help him feel better or get more done. And to whatever degree it makes him feel worse or get less done, Jim's conclusion is self-defeating.

Whether one of your conclusions is self-defeating or not is an entirely separate issue from whether your conclusion is true or not.

Some conclusions are verifiable. I have red hair. That's a fact. But sometimes you don't really *know* if a statement is true or false. For some statements, the question of true or false doesn't even *apply* (for example, an overblown generalization such as, "society is evil" can't be rationally argued one way or the other without being ridiculous).

But if a negative thought is impairing your ability, it is counterproductive to keep thinking it, whether its truth or falsity can ever be determined.

For example, let's say you're lying in bed obsessing over the thought, "I'm an insomniac and I will never again get a good night's sleep." The conclusion itself can keep you awake, so it is self-defeating to think it, whether it's true or false. It's a self-fulfilling prophesy.

Many pessimistic thoughts are like that: They are self-fulfilling and therefore not useful thoughts. Many of them aren't true or false. But they make themselves true by thinking them.

A woman wrote to me and said her grandmother always used to say, "Hell is right here on earth." That is an example of a demoralizing explanation of whatever setbacks she has experienced in her life. But is the explanation accurate? Is it true? You can't really say.

So the question then becomes: *Is the thought useful?* Is it helpful? Clearly the grandmother's conclusion about life, the assumption she made that "hell is right here on earth," produces a feeling of sadness, demoralization, and hopelessness. It would not help her overcome the challenges in her life. Not only that, but her feelings are *unhealthy*. And in fact, the grandmother was constantly grumpy and depressed.

With many of your conclusions, you can take away their power to influence you by simply realizing they aren't true. But if you can't determine the truth of a negative conclusion, then look to see whether it is self-defeating. If you don't know if it's true, but you know it is self-defeating, your confidence in your conclusion will diminish as soon as you realize that fact, and its ability to affect your feelings will diminish right along with it.

# 8. false implications

THIS "SCIENCE OF determination" calls for a very simple task: When you feel discouraged, write down the negative thoughts you're having, and then check them for validity. See if some of the thoughts you have are questionable.

When you discover a negative or demoralizing thought that you now realize is not valid, you will immediately feel better. You will feel less discouraged. Your sense of purpose and feelings of determination will be stronger. Your fighting spirit will return.

You don't need to memorize the 22 virus definitions, although it would be okay if you did. All you have to do, really, is *get a feel* for them.

The human brain isn't perfect, and it makes mistakes in its thinking. When you assume something disheartening, it is entirely possible your assumption is a mistake. It might be inaccurate, or based on weak evidence, or not the only possible way to interpret the circumstances. If you never question your assumption, your determination and your feeling of motivation will be weak because of that false assumption. You can be defeated in your mind just as thoroughly as you would be if your assumption was *true*.

So take the time when you feel demoralized (or not as motivated as you once were), and write down your explanations for your setbacks and then see if there is anything wrong with them. Look at the evidence you have for your negative assumptions. Is it enough evidence? Would it convince a jury?

Okay, let's say it would. But here's a new angle: Even if you have *plenty of evidence* for an explanation and even if it's the *only* explanation you can think of, what you think your explanation *implies* may be mistaken or unnecessarily self-defeating. *This* is the mind virus of "false implications."

For example, let's say you want "peace on earth." You're an activist, a protester, and you work toward a more peaceful world. But of course, you see the news and read reports of wars around the world. This is a setback. It makes you feel discouraged.

And what should you do when you feel discouraged? Write down your negative thoughts. Write down what you think *caused* the setback. So you write, "Violence is the human condition." That's your explanation of the setback.

You then try to see if there is anything wrong with your negative thought. First you look at the evidence, and discover that unfortunately, you have plenty of evidence. Wars have been fought since the beginning of history.

But then you look at the *implications* of your negative thought. The thought implies that 1) nothing can change it, and 2) that love and kindness are not also the human condition.

You realize that "nothing can change it" is probably not true. And it is true that love and kindness are also part of the human condition. Once you realize the implications are false (or at the very least, incomplete), the thought, "violence is the human condition" isn't as disheartening. Your motivation to work for peace returns when you realize the implications of your pessimistic conclusion didn't hold as much water as you originally thought.

It is rarely the circumstances by themselves that make you feel discouraged. It is your thoughts about the circumstances. If you discover that your thoughts are inaccurate or invalid, your discouragement will vanish. You'll feel more determination and motivation almost immediately.

Let's look at another example. John and his wife are arguing. They've had the same argument about the same thing since they've been married. And nothing seems to change. It is frustrating, and John feels discouraged. He doesn't think it's ever going to change. His stomach is twisted in a knot and he feels like he can't breathe. What should he do? He should use the antivirus for the mind, of course.

So he sits down and writes out what he thinks is *causing* the setback. He wants a happy marriage and this ongoing, irresolvable fight is the setback. It keeps ruining their affection for each other. What is causing this setback? He thinks, "I'm impatient. I have always been impatient. I'm just an impatient person."

This statement, this assumption of his, contains more than one thought-mistake, but let's just look at the *implications* of it. The implication is: He cannot become more patient. And that is probably not true. If he concentrated on becoming more patient, he would probably find ways and means.

If he talked with people he knew who were patient and asked them how they think about things, he is likely to find some good ideas to try. He could read some books on the subject.

If he looked into it, he would find lots of avenues he could pursue to develop more patience.

If these ongoing arguments with his wife are truly intolerable, John's question should be, "Even though I have always been impatient, *would I be willing* to change that seemingly fixed characteristic if it would make our marriage better?"

When you're looking at your own explanations of setbacks, look at the *evidence* for your demoralizing thoughts, but also look at the *implications* of your thoughts. If you discover the implications are false, you will cease feeling disheartened and your determination will come back.

Here's another example: A woman was depressed because she'd lost her job two years ago, and hadn't gotten another job since. She felt like a failure because she was still jobless after all this time.

Her explanation of her failure was: She didn't do well in job interviews.

Her therapist wanted to test this, so he did a mock interview with her, and the therapist agreed — she was terrible at being interviewed.

However, her conclusion was that because she interviewed so badly, she would never get a job. The therapist, on the other hand, concluded that since they now knew exactly what the problem was, getting a job has become possible. All she had to do was learn to interview well.

So they practiced and the therapist coached her to improve the way she presented herself and she got better. They rehearsed, did mockups, recorded the practice sessions and really worked on it.

At her very next interview, she was offered a job. That was ten years ago. She has been continually employed since then in a very competitive field.

Now look at what happened. Her explanation for her failure was *correct*. She made no thought-mistakes there. She thought she was a lousy interview, and she was. But she made a mistake in the *implication* she drew from that. She thought the fact that she wasn't good at interviewing implied she couldn't get hired. This implication is wrong, or at least you could draw a more productive implication from the same fact.

So when you're going through the process, writing down your demoralizing thoughts and checking them for thought-mistakes, go one step further. If you find a demoralizing thought and you know it's true, explore further. What demoralizing implications have you concluded about it? Are they *necessarily* true? Don't be so sure.

Consider any negative thought you have as automatically suspect. Really *look* at it because the consequences are significant.

## 9. choosing the worst possible explanation

THE REPUBLICANS won because they manipulated the election results. The air is polluted because nobody cares. The reason she left me is I'm a loser. These are all explanations of events. And of course these are not the only possible explanations for those events. In fact, with a little time, most people could come up with many alternative explanations, some of them more likely to be true and less likely to be demoralizing. But when you're feeling down, you are more likely to explain setbacks with the worst possible explanation. And this tends to make you feel even more demoralized.

In other words, the more disheartened you get, the more likely you are to choose the worst possible explanation, which can make discouragement a self-perpetuating, self-feeding, downward spiral.

What can you do about it? Simple: Notice you have chosen a dire explanation, realize it's not the only possible one, and make a list of other, less dire, more likely explanations. It always comes back to using the antivirus for your mind. Always do it in writing. It doesn't take long and it works like magic.

Write down what you think *caused* your setback. This is your "explanation" of the setback. Now find something wrong with that explanation. One thing that might be wrong — one possible thought-mistake — is assuming your explanation is the *only* valid one when it isn't. The solution is to make a list of possible alternative explanations. Think of something else (something less depressing) that explains the setback just as well.

For example, you start a new business, you're feeling enthusiastic, but after a few months, things aren't going as well as you'd hoped, and it slowly dawns on you it is going to take longer than you thought to make good money. This is a setback. Remember, a setback is anything that happens that you didn't want to happen. Or anything that doesn't happen that you wanted to happen.

So this is a setback: You're not making money as quickly as you thought.

You feel discouraged because you automatically explained the setback with the worst possible explanation, "People don't want my product." That's an explanation of the setback. But it's only one of *many* possible explanations. You try to come up with alternative explanations. What other reasons would explain why you aren't making as much money as you thought you would? You might write a list like this:

1.  I didn't know much about this business when I started, so my predictions about how fast things would happen were bound to be wrong.

2.  It might take a while for people to find out about my product.

3.  I didn't spend enough money on advertising.

4.  I spent money on the wrong kind of advertising.

5.  My original expectations were unrealistic.

6.  I'm just being impatient.

These are possible explanations of the setback. Any of these explanations would be less disheartening than the one you came up with first.

Which explanation do you choose? It depends. If one of them seems more right than the others, you can choose that one. But you also have the option of not choosing any. In truth, your setback was probably caused by more than one factor, and you may not know which ones.

As far as your feeling of discouragement is concerned, it doesn't really matter. As soon as you recognize your explanation isn't the only one possible, you will almost immediately feel your mood lifting. Your head will come out of the darkness and it will become easier to think of less catastrophic explanations than the first one you came up with. Your rising mood will start to work in your favor, creating an *upward* spiral.

## 10. false helplessness

MARTIN SELIGMAN, author of the book, *Learned Optimism*, has a different way of describing the possible mistakes we make in our explanations, although our lists, as well as the lists of cognitive therapists David Burns and Aaron Beck all cover the same ground but simply divide the ground differently.

The most important thought-mistake on Seligman's list, as I mentioned earlier, is deciding the cause of a setback is *unchangeable*. Seligman calls it "permanence."

You can probably see why the assumption is so devastating. It creates a feeling of helplessness and takes away any incentive you might have had to find a solution, solve the problem, or overcome the obstacle.

My wife, Klassy, and I started a policy — out of frustration at our lack of productive work getting done around here because we like to talk to each other so much — we decided to write from 10 AM until 1 PM. No eating. No email. No calls. Not even talking to each other. It worked great. We both saw tremendous production for about two weeks, but then I said I wanted a day off from it. Then we took another day off the following day. Then it was my birthday and we took another day off. Then it was two days before a vacation, so we prepared and figured we'd get back and start it up again. Then Klassy helped her sister move, and the next day she had a cold and slept in.

What do you do when *you* relapse — when a good plan fails? It depends on how you explain the failure and how willing you are to try again (and your willingness will be determined by how you explained the relapse).

We might have concluded, "We have no self-discipline." This is a "permanent" explanation (thinking of it as a character flaw). It is false helplessness. And conclusions about unchangeability are so demoralizing, they tend to become self-fulfilling prophesies.

They are self-fulfilling because if you think something cannot be changed, you have very little motivation to try to change it, which makes change very unlikely.

Scurvy is an historical example of this. When sailors first took to the sea in great numbers for long voyages, scurvy was very common. And it was a horrible way to die. Vitamin C is a vital component in connective tissue, and when you don't get any, the things holding you together start coming apart! Yuck!

Scurvy was a major setback. Not only did it prevent many exploratory and profit-making goals from being achieved, but of course, it prevented many sailors from gaining their goal of making it home alive!

Nobody knew what caused it at the time. In fact, the causes of scurvy were thought to be "infinite and unsearchable." (How is that for false helplessness?) James Lind eventually narrowed down the causes (and thus the cure) by 1753, and in so doing discovered the first vitamin. There was only one cause (lack of vitamin C), and it was "searchable," so the common explanation of the day was mistaken.

Anybody who believed the "infinite and unsearchable" explanation didn't find the remedy, and wouldn't have even tried.

Closer to home, when you decide the cause of one of your setbacks is permanent, your conclusion will demoralize you. This can easily devolve into depression.

Depression is defined primarily by negative thinking. And depression isn't on or off; it is a graduated scale from slightly down to completely incapacitated.

The size of the setback — the significance of it — determines how deep your depression will be. In other words the importance of the goal and the largeness of the setback will determine how big of a blow it will be.

But your explanations of the setback will determine how well you bounce back — how quickly, how completely, how easily you recover, pick yourself up, and move on.

For example, Jim and Sue lost their jobs from the same company on the same day, and they have two entirely different explanations for why they were laid off.

Jim thinks, "The economy is bad. That's why they laid me off."

Sue thinks, "They didn't lay off everyone. They must have chosen me because they noticed my heart wasn't in it."

Same circumstances, different explanation.

The consequences of their explanations are different too, and maybe in a different way than you think. Which do you think is a better explanation? Jim's explanation blames something outside himself. Sue's explanation makes it her "fault." But which helps more in recovering determination? Which will more quickly restore motivation? Which will help the most in accomplishing the goal of getting another job?

Jim feels defeated by his explanation and has no motivation to try to find another job. His explanation of the cause of the setback is widespread and out of his control (it was the economy).

Sue's explanation, however, may cause her to decide to get a job she really wants this time so she will really put her heart into it. Her explanation was more specific and more in her control.

Bouncing back quickly is not merely nice — it is consequential. When you are feeling demoralized and dispirited, problems are more likely to be overwhelming. Why? Because you are less capable when you feel bad. Metaphorically speaking, you are smaller (not able to accomplish as much, not as capable), so the problems seem larger in relation to you.

Anybody would be more easily overwhelmed if they were depressed. The same circumstances wouldn't seem overwhelming to the same person undepressed.

Helplessness is the feeling you get when your deliberate actions do not have any effect on the outcome. If your deliberate actions might, in fact, alter the way things turn out, then an explanation that says you have no influence is wrong. You have fallen victim to *false helplessness.*

This may be the most important mind virus to look for. A sense of helplessness will stop any further actions on your own behalf. If you can find that your feeling of helplessness is mistaken, it will totally change your outlook.

# 11. false hopelessness

"HUMANS WILL DESTROY the earth." Not only is this a negative guess, not only is it demoralizing, but it is false hopelessness. It is false in the sense that it contains too much certainty. Nobody knows what is going to happen in the future. And it is also false because something might be done in the meantime that could change how things turn out.

False hopelessness is a kind of cop out. Like the statement above, it gives you an excuse to not even try. I hear it all the time. People are convincing themselves of things like this because (at least in part) it absolves them of responsibility. They don't have to do anything because "nothing can be done." But by convincing themselves of false hopelessness, they also demoralize themselves unnecessarily.

You've heard the phrase, "It took all the fight out of me." One thing many people don't realize is that if you convince yourself of false hopelessness about, let's say, the future of the human race, that hopeless feeling soaks through and stains your whole life.

If you don't want to work toward ending world hunger, you can make that choice without deciding it cannot be done.

You're reading this right now because you have at least one strong goal. Keep your focus on that goal, and when it is accomplished, put your attention on the next goal.

In the meantime, do not defile your mind with false hopelessness about anything. When you don't know, admit you don't know, and leave it at that.

## 12. shoulds and musts

"I SHOULD BE a nicer person." "People shouldn't treat me that way." "The world should be fairer." These kinds of statements are called *imperatives*. They are also called "should statements" by David Burns. The late Albert Ellis focused on this thought-mistake more than any other. He called it "musterbation." Ellis concentrated on it for a good reason. It's the source of a great deal of unnecessary negative emotion.

In an interview, Ellis explained how he got *himself* out of an upset.

1.  First he says to himself, "I'm creating this (my distress)."

2.  Then he asks, "What am I telling myself?"

3.  Finally he looks for commands and demands: "Things should not be this way, the other person should not act that way, I should not feel this way, etc."

Ellis focused on shoulds and musts because he found by long experience that these really get people in trouble. It's always a good thought-mistake to look for.

Ellis was not only an innovator and teacher, but he used this stuff on his own therapy clients since the 1950s. His experience showed him he could usually go right to the heart of the matter quickly by first searching for shoulds and musts.

Once you recognize the shoulds and oughts and musts you use on yourself, and once you realize they are merely *preferences*, it takes away the intensity of your negative feelings and you are left with mild disappointment, simple frustration, or concern — rather than sadness, anger, or fear.

Ellis began by assuming right off the bat that if you've got a problem, the source of it is "musterbation."

For example, you might present a problem in a therapy session that you are ashamed or embarrassed about something. His very *first* assumption is that the source of your distress is you are thinking either, "I *must* be loved by everyone," or "I *must* achieve greatness," or both. And he would probably be right. From either of those two underlying musts, you can easily become embarrassed or ashamed when someone does not seem to think you're wonderful, or when you did something that wasn't totally great.

Ellis would then teach you that there is no reason to continue believing you *must* be loved or achieve greatness. Sure, it would be *nice*, but it isn't necessary to existence, and *thinking it's necessary* makes you miserable.

## 13. misplacing responsibility

THIS MISTAKE CAN GO either way. You can take too *much* responsibility for something, or too *little*. Either will cause you more distress and discouragement than the circumstances call for. If you blame yourself for something that really wasn't your fault, you feel bad unnecessarily. If you blame someone *else* for something *you* were responsible for, you impede your ability to improve the situation. If you don't take credit for something you could legitimately be proud of, you miss out on personal pride (and it will tend to sap your motivation over time).

Go through the process of writing down your thoughts when you are demoralized or upset, and "misplacing responsibility" is bound to show up as one of your mistakes.

In the antivirus for your mind, we're *not* trying to be positive. We're trying to be *accurate*. So if you find you have a thought like, "It's all my fault," you have to really look at that. If it really *is* all your fault, you have not made a mistake. But if you look at it honestly and realize it isn't entirely your fault, your distress will ease right on the spot.

## 14. focusing too narrowly

ON OTHER LISTS of thought-mistakes, this is called "filtering" or "negative filter." It means focusing on a negative detail and ignoring other parts of the situation that might not be so bad. It could also be called "ig-noring the good."

For example, let's say my wife says something that seems hostile to me, and I get upset by it, focusing on what I perceive to be her hostility and ignoring the fact that we've spent the last two hours in a great conver-sation, and also ignoring the fact that immediately prior to her being hostile, I said something insulting!

So in other words, my upsetting feelings are being generated by focusing too narrowly.

When you're looking at your negative statement, look for this kind of tunnel vision, because it is a *mistake*. You're leaving out other facts that would make your explanation of the situation a lot less upsetting. It's a mistake by omission.

What you *see* may not be a mistake, but you're filtering out other facts that would ease your suffering or eliminate your feeling of discouragement.


## 15. harmful judging

YOU HAVE TO MAKE judgments all day long. You couldn't function without exercising your judgment. But this same skill can be harmful if it isn't done care-fully. You already know judging others can harm *them*, but we're concerned here with the kind of judgment that harms *you*. It weakens you in some way or demor-alizes you.

For example, let's say you have just started a bus-iness. You need to make four appointments per day to succeed. But you just don't get around to making the phone calls you need to make, and you're starting to feel frustrated and disappointed in yourself.

These are negative emotions. What will you *always* do from now on when you feel any negative emotions? The antivirus for your mind of course!

What do you do when your computer starts malfunctioning? When it starts moving slowly or doing something strange, you do a virus scan, right? You first find out if you have something on your hard drive interfering with your computer.

Same with your own mind. When you feel a negative emotion, it might be caused by a mind virus (a thought-mistake). So go through the simple process of writing down what you're thinking and then looking at those thoughts and finding the mistakes.

So you haven't been making your four calls a day. You feel demoralized. You write down your thoughts:

1. I don't have enough time.

2. I have no self-discipline.

3. I'm a loser.

These are your reasons for the setback. These are your explanations of your failure to make those calls. Number 3 is harmful judging. On other lists it is called "labeling" or "mislabeling." You're judging yourself harshly and it makes you feel bad. The thought, "I'm a loser," makes you *feel* like a loser. Does that help? Will that help you make your four calls a day? No. In fact, it will make it *harder* for you to make those calls! You are harming yourself with your judging.

Once you realize this, you will naturally be more wary of thinking this thought in the future, and maybe you'll catch yourself thinking it and have a little argument in your head about it. And every time you do, the thought has less power. It will have less authority over you. When it occurs to you, it will be easier for you to dismiss it.

And I should say here that once you have dismissed a thought, you will not necessarily be cured of ever making that thought-mistake again. The mind has habits. But by noticing the thought and recognizing it as a mistake, that thought won't so easily bring you down in the future. It has been discredited. It will be *easier* to dismiss in the future. You may eventually stop thinking it altogether.

If you do not examine your thoughts like this, however, you could try for years to *force* yourself to make those calls, while still habitually thinking you are a loser when you fail. Your path would be harder, and your thought-mistake could become a self-fulfilling prophesy.

Take my advice: Don't take the long road full of suffering. Root out your thought-mistakes and get back to work feeling good. Seek out and find those viruses lurking in your mind. Just finding them and seeing that you were mistaken about them dissipates their power. What you will have left is a good attitude, determination, and a strong feeling of motivation to accomplish the goals you really want.

## 16. asking unanswerable questions

JUST BECAUSE YOU can ask a question doesn't mean it has an answer. What's north of the North Pole? What's the best decision you could ever make? What did your face look like before your parents were born? Those are essentially *meaningless* questions, even though they are well-formed grammatically.

The same is true for questions like, "What are they thinking about me?" or "Why aren't people buying my product?" These questions are not answerable from inside your head, so they will go round and round, upsetting you and getting you nowhere. Those two questions can only be answered by asking someone *else*.

What about this question: "Why am I so committed to failure?" That may or may not be answerable, but I'll tell you this: You'll never know if you have the "right" answer. A much more productive thing to do with "why questions" like those is to ask *how* instead. How can I succeed? What would be the smartest way to proceed from here? What steps would I need to take next?

Be careful with the questions you ask yourself. Questions have a way of generating trains of thought, so which questions you ask can make a big difference. Ideally you would ask questions that produce effective, helpful, constructive, and productive trains of thought.

When you feel discouraged by a setback, keep your eye out for unanswerable questions and replace them with questions you *can* answer, such as, "What will I do today to move my goal forward?"

## 17. bias for confirmation

RESEARCHERS HAVE FOUND that our brains automatically seek evidence to *confirm* rather than disconfirm an already existing conclusion — whether we have any stake in it or not.

When you allow yourself to come to a conclusion that you aren't very organized, for example, you'll see and remember things you do that confirms your conclusion even if you don't want it to be true. And you'll ignore times you were well-organized because they don't confirm anything; they disconfirm.

When you decide your spouse is a slob, you will notice and remember (clearly) the times your spouse acted like a slob, and you'll be more likely to ignore or explain away the times your spouse was neat and clean. This bias for confirmation can ruin your mood and alter your relationships for the worse far more often than reality warrants.

Does this sound familiar? You get a flat tire and you think, "The day is ruined!" That's giving up. That's defeatism. That's feeling helpless. Because of your bias for confirmation, *your decision* about the day can actually ruin the whole day.

Another version of this is, "Things are going badly." What's wrong with that statement? Can you tell? When you say things are going badly, you are projecting the badness into the future and defeating yourself ahead of time! How about, "Things have gone badly up to this point." Much better. It's more specific, more accurate, and it opens your mind to ways you might change your trajectory.

Coming to a conclusion prematurely alters your perception to some degree — at least it alters what you notice and remember — so what you see agrees with your conclusions. It's a natural, built-in flaw of the human brain.

And telling people your conclusions makes it even worse. In an experiment, people were asked to determine the length of a line. One group was told to decide how long the line was *in their heads*; another group was told to *write it* on a Magic Pad (pads for children that erase what's written when you lift up the top sheet) and then erase it before anyone saw it; and a third group was told to write their conclusions on a piece of paper, sign it, and give it to the researcher.

Then the subjects were given information indicating that their first conclusion was wrong, and then they were given an opportunity to change their decision. Those who decided in their heads changed their conclusions the easiest; those who wrote it on the Magic Pad were more reluctant to change their minds; and those who declared their conclusions publicly remained the most convinced their first conclusion was correct.

Their feeling of certainty was an illusion; it wasn't related to their conclusion's *accuracy*. It was being influenced by another factor — how public they had made their conclusions.

Be careful about coming to conclusions too quickly — especially in public. Slow yourself down before you conclude anything negative or pessimistic. Remind yourself that your feeling of certainty might not mean anything. When your conclusion is giving you negative feelings, skepticism can make you feel better and act more sanely.

Confucius said wisdom was "when you know a thing, to recognize that you know it, and when you do not know a thing, to recognize that you do not know it." That almost sounds stupid, but look around you and observe how often people do not do this. Including you and me.

I was lying down for a nap yesterday and noticed my back hurt. I immediately thought it was because I'd been sitting at the computer so much. This made me slightly despondent because I still had a lot of work I wanted to do on the computer.

Then I checked that explanation and realized I really didn't know what caused my back pain.

My uncertainty opened the possibility that maybe it's not sitting, but *how* I sit (my posture). The uncertainty, then, did two good things. It made me feel less discouraged by the back pain, and more open to seeking better answers than the first thing that popped into my head.

Uncertainty can be good. We often think thoughts with more certainty than is justified. A while back, a little story circulated on the internet that was supposedly a radio conversation "released by the Chief of Naval Operations." Here's how it went:

**Radio Number One:** Please divert your course 15 degrees to the North to avoid a collision.

**Radio Number Two:** Recommend you divert YOUR course 15 degrees to South to avoid a collision.

**Number One:** This is the captain of a U.S. Navy ship. I say again, divert YOUR course.

**Number Two:** No. I say again, you divert YOUR course.

**Number One:** THIS IS THE AIRCRAFT CARRIER ENTERPRISE. WE ARE A LARGE WARSHIP OF THE U.S. NAVY. DIVERT YOUR COURSE NOW!

**Number Two:** This is a lighthouse. Your call.

I doubt if this incident ever happened, but it illustrates the value of uncertainty. The Navy captain concluded he was talking to a stubborn and ignorant person who was willfully ignoring an important order. He jumped to a conclusion quickly and his anger narrowed his focus too much to reconsider. Most of us have made similar mistakes.

Learn to suspend judgment. Learn to delay coming to conclusions when you can.

But, you might be thinking, if you must know a lot before coming to a conclusion, you won't form many opinions. Yes, that's right. You should do your best — against your own natural propensity — to leave your opinion undecided when you don't know enough to decide correctly.

When you feel bad, ask yourself:

1. "What am I thinking that's giving me these feelings?"

2. "Is this absolutely, positively true?" Ask this question of every negative thought in your mind. "Do I *know for a fact* it's true?"

If you do this, your emotions will fit the reality of your situation. If it's true that you think things with more certainty than is justified by the facts, then your certainty is probably discouraging, upsetting, or demoralizing you *unnecessarily*.

In 1940, Slavomir Rawicz was sent to a Siberian prison camp for twenty-five years. He eventually did the impossible and escaped. Then he did the impossible again and walked 4000 miles through Siberia, across the Gobi desert, and over the Himalayas, all as a wanted fugitive, and finally made it to India and freedom.

But all that was to come later. While he was still imprisoned, he was asking around, seeing if he could find anyone who might be willing to come with him.

"If I could one day think up a plan of escape," he asked a friend of his in the prison, "would you come with me?"

"No," his friend replied, "I would come with you if there was a chance, but the snow and the cold would kill us before we could get anywhere, even if the Russians didn't catch us."

Here was certainty about a demoralizing conclusion — and the conclusion was wrong. We now know that he *did* escape, the Russians *didn't* catch them, and the snow and the cold *didn't* kill them. In Thomas Gilovich's excellent book, *How We Know What Isn't So*, he wrote,

> Perhaps the most general and most important mental habit to instill is an appreciation of the folly of trying to draw conclusions from incomplete and unrepresentative evidence. An essential corollary of this appreciation should be an awareness of how often our everyday experience presents us with biased samples of information.

Have you ever drawn conclusions from incomplete evidence? When I was making cold calls for radio interviews, I made about fifteen calls for every interview I landed. When I called, I usually left a voice mail.

They'd call back and grill me. When I first started doing it, this made me feel bad. So what did I do? I looked into my thinking to find mistakes. I used the most powerful mental tool known to Man: *The Antivirus For Your Mind*. These are some of the thoughts I had:

- "This is too hard."
- "I'm never going to make it."
- "Nobody is interested."

- "Nobody cares about improving their lives."
- "I can't take the strain."

After I wrote them down, I realized these conclusions weren't necessarily true. My negative feelings subsided and my success rate improved (I came across better because I was in a better mood).

When I first started public speaking, I had to do the same thing. My explanation for why I couldn't be a public speaker was *false helplessness*: "I'm constitutionally shy, always have been, always will be." I was overgeneralizing (mind viruses often overlap each other). I thought, "I'm a shy person" rather than "I'm shy in certain circumstances." Or better yet, "I'm only nervous because it is unfamiliar."

Ever since I was nineteen, I had wanted to give public speeches, *but I knew I couldn't*. Some people can, I thought, and some can't. I was one who couldn't. That's a permanent explanation — an overgeneralization.

"Permanent" explanations can stop you as effectively as a 90-foot wall of concrete. You can see this very clearly in true survival stories. It is interesting to see what people do in their minds that helps them make it home alive. One common denominator is they do not overgeneralize. They don't decide it is hopeless. They don't say, "Nothing has worked yet, so nothing will *ever* work." They retain a glimmer of uncertainty about their own pessimistic assumptions, and so they keep trying, and that's what saves them.

It would be equally instructive to know what went through the minds of those who *didn't* survive. No doubt some of them made pessimistic overgeneralizations that prevented them from taking actions that might have saved them.

People can even make all-or-nothing assumptions about their own attitude. They are "just not a cheerful person." Or they can't become a *perfectly* cheerful person so they don't do *anything* that would improve their moods a little.

I remember Martin Seligman saying we don't really need to cultivate pessimism, however useful it may occasionally be, because each person has ups and downs, and during the downs everyone gets plenty of pessimistic views of their life.

Temporary pessimism may be useful, which means you don't have to be positive all the time. In fact, it might be a bad thing if you were.

If you think you should *never* be in a bad mood, that's all-or-nothing thinking. It's also musterbating (using shoulds and musts).

I would bet many "positive" people feel that they must be positive all the time, and that somehow when they're in a bad mood or grumpy or pessimistic, it is bad and wrong and invalidates them.

The idea that "it's okay and maybe even *good* to be pessimistic once in a while" is an optimistic view of pessimism. You can even feel good about feeling bad. You can be positive about being negative!

If you can't change the thing itself, you can still change how you deal with it, how you respond to it, what you do with it. Some things are not changeable, but you can still do something about it (to compensate).

Anyway, as interesting and entertaining as all this may be, I've gotten off the point a little. We're talking about the thought-mistake "bias for confirmation."

Whatever you think or conclude or decide, it can have an influence on how you perceive your future, and *that* can have an influence on how motivated or demoralized you are.

So pay attention to what you are concluding and never conclude something negative or discouraging unless you are one hundred percent certain of it, and that will rarely be the case.

## 18. using emotions as evidence

SOMETIMES, ONLY BECAUSE we haven't really thought about it, we make really dumb mistakes in our thinking. For example, "I really feel afraid. That must mean there is something to be afraid of."

This is called *emotional reasoning.* It is fairly common and fairly foolish. Our emotions are at least partly a *response* to our thoughts. We can't take them as *evidence* to justify our thoughts.

One woman I know is afraid of flying. She gets anxious while she is on a plane. When I talked to her about it, she said, "Something bad might happen while we're in the air."

"What makes you think so?" I asked her.

"I feel afraid. The fear is my body warning me of danger." This is an example of using emotions as evidence.

Sometimes you may get a feeling about someone or some situation and it is evidence of your *perception* of that moment and that situation, and as Gavin de Becker argues in his excellent book, *The Gift of Fear*, if you're smart, you will listen to that kind of fear. It may save your life.

But if *every time* you get on a plane you feel fear, and yet you continue to fly safely, then your fear is *not* evidence. Your fear is a response to your thoughts, which you should write down and argue with.


## 19. dismissing facts

WHEN YOU FEEL down because of a setback, you will tend to make more mistakes in your thinking, which just makes you feel worse. Negative emotions can create a kind of tunnel vision where you focus on all the things you don't like and ignore the positives. For example, you make a proposal to three people in a row and they all turn you down. You feel discouraged because you're thinking the idea is no good.

But last Wednesday five out of five said *yes*. When you feel demoralized by a setback, that is exactly the kind of evidence you will dismiss or forget. Even if you remember it, you might dismiss it by thinking, "I got lucky that day."

People do this sort of thing all the time. When someone compliments you, what do you think? Many people will think, "They're just saying that to be nice." They dismissed something positive. It is entirely possible they *were* just trying to be nice. But it's also possible they mean it. And it's also possible they're nice *and* they mean it. You don't know. So why pick the negative one?

The fact is, the person said something nice. The fact is, it is possible they meant it. Never dismiss facts, especially when it leaves you feel bad unnecessarily.


## 20. ignoring alternatives

USUALLY SEVERAL FACTORS influence the outcome of any given event. You may have latched onto the most demoralizing factor and decided that's what caused it. Look for alternative (and equally likely) influencing factors. The more you find, the less demoralizing any one of them will be.

As Martin Seligman wrote: If you did poorly on a test, many factors could have contributed to that outcome. You may have been tired, the test might've been unusually difficult, the other students might have done exceptionally well (so they raised the grading curve), you may not have studied as much as you should have, the professor may have graded unfairly, you might not be very smart, and so on.

All of those factors are possible causes of the setback (your poor grade is the setback in this case). Some people leap to the most demoralizing conclusion and fixate on that, ignoring the other possible causes, debilitating themselves and feeling bad when it is entirely avoidable (and penalty-free).

That was a lot to pack into one paragraph, so let me explain it a little better. First you run into a setback, which means something didn't go the way you had hoped. And you feel let down by it. You feel demoralized. The bad feeling causes you to focus on whatever explanation for the setback popped into your head first. Sometimes this will be the most dire explanation. You focus on that one and ignore the fact that many different causes may have influenced how things turned out. Many of those other causes wouldn't make you feel so bad, but you are ignoring them.

For example, let's say I start a blog and I write some stuff, and I see more and more people coming to my site, and everything is great, but all of a sudden my traffic starts to go *down!* This is a setback. Let's say I feel upset about it.

I think to myself, "They've all come and looked at my site and rejected it. I am a lousy blogger." I ignore several other possible influencing factors like this is a holiday weekend or random variation or whatever.

But I am fixated on my dire and catastrophic explanation for my setback, and it really gets me down. Why? Because I have committed the thought-mistake of *ignoring alternatives*. The virus has infected my mind.

What should I do? Why, of course: Put myself right with the antivirus for your mind and restore my determination as quickly as possible.

## 21. assuming

OF COURSE, MOST thought-mistakes fall into the general category of "assuming." But it is a good thing to look for on its own. Most of us know *assuming* is a dangerous business, and yet most of us do it anyway. It is hard to catch yourself doing it, because of course, you assume what you assume to be true is true. What is there to catch?

Throughout your personal history, some of your biggest mistakes probably stemmed from an assumption you made that was mistaken. And throughout human history in general, you can easily see the march of progress as a continual discovery that one assumption after another was wrong.

The medical treatment of George Washington is a good example.

It started out as a sore throat. Washington had a cold. So he was treated with the usual procedure: *Bloodletting.* Why was that the usual procedure? Because Galen of Pergamon, a prominent Roman "physician" recommended it sixteen hundred years before, and Galen was so well-known and well-respected, and his practices and theories were so well-established that the doctors in Washington's time *assumed* Galen must be right.

Of course it didn't help. In fact, his condition got worse and he began having trouble breathing. He was famous and wealthy, so he was ministered by the very "best" doctors. They put ground beetles on his throat to cause blisters (in order to pull out "bad vapors"). Then they gave him laxatives to purge his bowels. They also kept up the bloodletting for several days.

To you and me, it is no surprise that Washington went into a coma and then died. You could say he died of assumption.

When you are looking at the statements you have written down, go through them asking of each, "Does this statement contain an assumption? Have I assumed something to be true that I may not know for sure?" Catch as many as you can.

## 22. negative bias

WHY WOULD ANYONE focus on the *negative* aspect of a situation? Why would anyone dwell on the most *upsetting* aspects of circumstances? Why would anyone think depressing thoughts, knowing those thoughts are likely to make them depressed? Do people *want* to feel bad?

No.

You, me, and everyone else wants to be happy, but we're all under the influence of four powerful negative biases.

Really the driving force underpinning all of the other thought-mistakes are these four negative biases. The four biases are:

1. The brain's negative bias

2. Communication's negative bias

3. Reality's negative bias

4. The media's negative bias

These four biases drain away your life force, much in the same way as a lamprey — a fish with a suction cup for a mouth that attaches itself to other fish and drinks their blood. When that fish is dead, the lamprey lets go and finds another fish.

Lampreys are a good metaphor for the devastating impact negative emotions have on people. Negativity has a way of attaching itself to your mind, draining you of your health and ability — not metaphorically, but literally.

Negative emotions can contribute to heart disease and strokes, encourage the development of cancer, and even weaken your bones. Negative ways of thinking and perceiving the world can take away your creativity, your persistence, and your ability to achieve your goals. Negative emotions undermine your relationships, ruin your sense of humor, and impede your ability to solve problems. And they interfere with your memory.

A negative bias is a lamprey of the mind, a deadly parasite, and it uses your lifeblood, your energy, your mind, to breed and spread to other minds, using and destroying life force wherever it goes.

Let's go into some detail about the four negative biases.

**1. The brain:** Your brain reacts more strongly to negative information than it does to positive information. Threatening images capture your attention more compellingly than pleasant images. When your mind is not otherwise engaged, it has a tendency to drift randomly until an upsetting thought occurs. Then it'll stop drifting and think about the thing that upsets you.

Because of the brain's stronger reaction to (and greater fixation on) negative images and thoughts, the naturally-occurring thought-mistakes brains are prone to produce pessimism, cynicism, and defeatism, all three of which are self-defeating and counter-productive.

**2. Communication:** Because of the media and the pressures of social interaction, negativity has become chic. For social reasons, people will often withhold good news and share bad news. And a prominent topic of everyday conversations has an inevitably negative tone: Talking about grievances.

You and everyone else on this planet are compelled by your own biology to *gossip* — to share your complaints about other people, to listen to their complaints about other people, and to sympathize with the complainer.

On top of all this, your most significant goals have a good chance of being stomped on by well-meaning friends and family.

This makes any conversation an opportunity for "lampreys" to invade your mind.

**3. Reality:** It is usually easier to notice and remember something going wrong than something going right. This leads to pessimistic (and false) conclusions like, "My boss is *always* on my back," or "My wife *never* wants to do what I want."

Reality's negative bias works in several different ways. Sometimes no matter what decision you make, things are going to turn out badly. Under certain circumstances, the cutthroat behavior of others encourages nice people to be more cutthroat just to compete.

To make all this even worse, once reality displays its negative bias, it is natural to form negative conclusions that then function like self-fulfilling prophesies as your mind automatically looks for evidence to confirm your conclusions. Result: A tendency to become more pessimistic, cynical, and defeatist as you get more experience dealing with reality.

**4. Media:** Because of the brain's negative bias — combined with the intense competition between media outlets — producers and advertisers constantly exploit your natural reaction to threats of danger. The unfortunate side-effect is that the media is filled with pessimism-producing content.

And they use all the knowledge at their disposal (which is considerable) to keep you glued to the screen longer than you want to be, absorbing a distorted view of the world as a far more dangerous and depressing place than it really is.

The negative biases function like a lamprey attached to your mind, draining you of aliveness — sapping your strength and determination, impairing your health, and weakening your ability.

But with the antivirus for your mind — with the simple technique of doing an explanation-check every time you feel bad — you can bring back the determination, the positive attitude, the openness, the love, the happiness, the accomplishment, and the self-expressive exuberance that was once native to your mind.

# ABOUT THE AUTHOR

Adam Khan blogs at adamlikhan.com and podcasts at The Adam Bomb. He's the author of the books, *Self-Help Stuff That Works*, *Principles For Personal Growth* (now being used as a textbook for a college course in San Diego), *What Difference Does It Make: How the Sexes Differ and What You Can Do About It*, *How to Change the Way You Look at Things*, *Cultivating Fire: How to Keep Your Motivation White Hot*, *Direct Your Mind*, *Fill Your Tank With Freedom*, *Slotralogy*, and *Self-Reliance, Translated*.

Adam has been published in *Prevention Magazine*, *Cosmopolitan*, *Body Bulletin*, *Your Personal Best Newsletter*, *Wisdom*, *Think and Grow Rich Newsletter*, the *Success Strategies* newsletter, and he was a regular columnist for *At Your Best* (a Rodale Press publication) for seven years where his monthly column was voted the readers' favorite. He has been a regular columnist for Josh Hind's *Let's Talk Motivation* newsletter and nine other ezines. He's had his work reprinted all over the internet and in others' books all over the world. You can write to him at adamkhan@usa.com.

# PERSISTENCE AND DETERMINATION ARE OMNIPOTENT

WHEN YOU RUN into obstacles on the way to an important goal, and you feel your motivation starting to fade, or if people have been telling you you're foolish to keep trying, I urge you to watch the movie, *Lorenzo's Oil.* It's a true story of a husband and wife (Augusto and Michaela Odone) and their five year-old boy, Lorenzo.

They were a happy family who moved to the U.S. after living for a while in the Comoros Islands (an archipelago of volcanic islands off the southeast coast of Africa).

Lorenzo began having some behavioral problems, so they took him to one doctor after another, trying to get a diagnosis. Nobody seemed to know what was wrong with him.

Finally they found a doctor who did the right kind of tests. The doctor sat the parents down in a quiet room and gravely told them the diagnosis: "Your son has a fatal disease. He might live another two years, but during that time, the white matter of his brain will slowly liquefy, and then he will die. There is no treatment for this disease. Nothing can be done about it."

They were at the best facility they could find. The tests were thorough and extensive, and there was no mistake: Lorenzo has a disease called adrenoleukodystrophy (known simply as ALD).

What would *you* do if you were given this diagnosis for your child? They were, of course, devastated by the news. No matter how well-schooled you are in the antivirus for your mind, news like that will knock you down, at least at first.

Very little was known about ALD at the time, but Augusto (Lorenzo's father) started reading about it. He found the progression of the disease unthinkably horrible. Kids go blind and deaf, become autistic, lose their ability to speak, become paraplegic, have seizures, and so on over a period of two years. And then they die.

And nobody knew how to stop it.

Augusto and Michaela were plunged into a dark despair that would be hard to imagine. When anyone hits a setback, demoralization is almost always the first response. The only question is, "How quickly will you recover your fighting spirit?" How soon, if ever, will you regain your determination?

The answer depends entirely on how you explain the setback to yourself. If the Odones accepted the doctors' certainty, they would have given up on their son. They would have felt helpless and depressed.

But they decided there *must* be a way.

In other words, the setback was: Lorenzo has ALD. The explanation the doctors gave was: It's a fatal disease without a cure. It is permanent and unchangeable and we are certain about this.

That's a demoralizing assertion, and it makes at least four thought-mistakes: *overcertainty, negative guessing, self-defeating conclusions,* and *false hopelessness.*

Many people felt sorry for the Odones because the couple were obviously living on "false hope" (by deciding there must be a way). But if you look at the doctor's conclusion (there is no cure for ALD) you can easily see it was a premature conclusion. It was *not* a certainty that a cure was impossible. And it was unnecessarily demoralizing to say it with any certainty.

The Odone's explanation of the setback was not demoralizing. They believed the cure had not been found...*yet.* And they decided to see if they could help find the cure. Their explanation was the opposite of demoralizing — it was intensely motivating.

Even if they *wanted* to do something about it, many people wouldn't try because of *another* set of demoralizing beliefs: "Who am I to think I could help? I'm an ordinary person. How could I find a cure if all these doctors and researchers haven't found one?"

But the Odones thought differently. Augusto said to Michaela, "What did we do when we first arrived in Comoros? We *read* about it. We read about their culture, their history, their laws. That's what we need to do now. We don't know enough about this disease."

So they went to libraries and started reading as if their son's life depended on it. They stayed up late and got up early. They read books on biochemistry, biology, neurology. They read microfiche, pursued references, talked to researchers, and followed every clue they could find. They shared with each other what they were learning and what ideas they came up with, they argued with each other, and they kept trying.

*Why did they keep trying?*

This is the crucial question. They kept trying and stayed motivated because the way they explained their setback to themselves set them on fire with determination and commitment. Please remember that. When you feel demoralized by a setback, look at your explanations. Use the antivirus for your mind to protect and preserve and even enhance your feelings of motivation.

They discovered several researchers in different places working on the disease, but working in isolation from each other. The Odones thought they might speed up the process of discovery by funding a symposium, so they did. They got all the experts together in one room to discuss ALD. They thought maybe pooling their insights would help them find a new approach.

The Odones were trying to find a way. And they were urgent because the clock was ticking. Every day their son was losing more myelin (the protective sheath that covers the neurons in his brain). Lorenzo was going blind, couldn't speak, and was no longer able to feed himself.

## Lorenzo's Oil

At the symposium, in a conversation between scientists who each brought different pieces of the puzzle to the table, they concluded a particular oil might help. The Odones tracked down a manufacturer who could make it, and tried it on their boy. Their goal was to keep his level of long-chain fatty acids low. Those were the acids destroying his myelin.

The oil helped some, but not enough. They did more reading and found another line of possibility. They needed another oil extraction of a different kind but it couldn't be made legally in the U.S. So they found a chemist in England who could do it.

And the combination of the two oils *achieved* the goal! The level of fatty-acids in Lorenzo's blood became normal.

The oil is now used as a treatment for boys with ALD (girls don't get the disease) and if it's started early enough, it can stop the disease completely in many of them, allowing them to lead normal lives.

Lorenzo, however, did not return to normal. He had lost too much myelin. But he recovered some of his functions (including his eyesight) and is now *over thirty years old.*

Have the Odones given up? Of course not! They started The Myelin Project, aimed at finding a way to "re-myelinate" neurons. It has already been successfully done in dogs.

The movie is one of the most inspiring stories I've ever seen. If you would like to see a demonstration of determination in action, if you would like to see a real-life example of the power of persistence, if you would like to put the difficulty of your own goals into perspective, watch *Lorenzo's Oil.*

## The 22 Virus Definitions

I'm putting the list at the very back of the book so you can always easily refer to it:

1. exaggerating
2. overgeneralizing
3. oversimplifying
4. extremism
5. overcertainty
6. negative guessing
7. self-defeating conclusions
8. false implications
9. choosing the worst possible explanation
10. false helplessness
11. false hopelessness
12. shoulds and musts
13. misplacing responsibility
14. focusing too narrowly
15. harmful judging
16. asking unanswerable questions
17. bias for confirmation
18. using emotions as evidence
19. dismissing facts
20. ignoring alternatives
21. assuming
22. negative bias